HOCKEY HALL *of* FAME
BOOK *of*
JERSEYS

HOCKEY HALL *of* FAME
BOOK *of*
JERSEYS

STEVE MILTON

HOCKEY HALL *of* FAME

FIREFLY BOOKS

A FIREFLY BOOK

Published by Firefly Books Ltd. 2012

First printing

Publisher Cataloging-in-Publication Data (U.S.)
Milton, Steve.
     Hockey Hall of Fame book of jerseys / Steve Milton.
[192] p. : col. ill. ; cm.
Includes index.
Summary: Famous and significant jerseys and sweaters from the Hockey Hall of Fame's collection, game-worn by premier players during their greatest moments.
ISBN-13: 978-1-77085-103-0
1. Hockey – Equipment and supplies – History.   2. Hockey Hall of Fame – Collectibles – Pictorial works. 3. Hockey – History – Miscellanea.
I. Title.
796.962/0284 dc23   GV847.M568 2012

Library and Archives Canada Cataloguing in Publication
Milton, Steve
        Hockey Hall of Fame book of jerseys / Steve Milton.
Includes index.
ISBN 978-1-77085-103-0
        1. Hockey--Equipment and supplies--History. 2. Hockey--Equipment and supplies--History--Pictorial works. 3. Hockey Hall of Fame--Collectibles--Pictorial works. 4. Hockey players--History--Miscellanea. 5. Hockey--History--Miscellanea.
I. Hockey Hall of Fame II. Title.
GV847.M54 2012   796.962028'4   C2012-902190-3

Published in the United States by
Firefly Books (U.S.) Inc.
P.O. Box 1338, Ellicott Station
Buffalo, New York 14205

Published in Canada by
Firefly Books Ltd.
66 Leek Crescent
Richmond Hill, Ontario L4B 1H1

Photographs: Hal Roth Photography/HalRoth.ca
Cover and interior design: Jamie Hodgson/studio34design.ca
Creative Direction/Editor: Steve Cameron

Printed in China

The publisher gratefully acknowledges the financial support for our publishing program by the Government of Canada through the Canada Book Fund as administered by the Department of Canadian Heritage.

PAGE TWO IMAGE: A close-up photograph of the crest of Bobby Clarke's Flin Flon Bombers jersey. Clarke wore this jersey during the 1968–69 season, in which the Bombers won the Western Canadian Junior Hockey League title.

Tab indicates the year a player was inducted to the Hockey Hall of Fame.

CONTENTS

INTRODUCTION

BY PHIL PRITCHARD

I S IT CALLED A JERSEY? Or is it a sweater? It's a great question that has been debated among hockey circles for years. No matter the answer, one thing is for sure: the Hockey Hall of Fame prides itself on having the world's premier collection of hockey uniforms.

The concept of the Hockey Hall of Fame started in the 1940s when some of the prominent figures in hockey began collecting game-worn articles from players and teams. Although there wasn't a building until 1961, this early groundwork paved the way for the first collections that appeared at the Canadian National Exhibition grounds. Bobby Hewitson and Maurice "Lefty" Reid, along with their small staff, deserve a great deal of credit for their foresight. Collecting jerseys was one thing, but following milestones and tracking uniform styles and logo changes was not a simple task.

Today our vision of the Hockey Hall of Fame remains very similar to the one conceived by Bobby and Lefty, it is just more diverse. As the game has grown, so have the styles and designs that make up hockey's uniforms. Canada's gift to the world is now played in over 70 countries, and while some nations may only have a handful of club teams, many have well-established minor and professional leagues — with each team sporting a different uniform. Ideally we'd love to have an item from every team that has ever played, and as we build our collection we never tire of adding new pieces.

Donations come from all over. Sometimes we'll receive help securing items for donation from people such as Pierre Trudeau and Marc Juteau of Classic Auctions, or Barry Meisel and Stu Oxenhorn of the MeiGray Group. Longtime collector Allan Stitt has also kept his eyes and ears open for us.

Oftentimes, teams or players will go out of their way to donate items to us. After the 2008–09 playoffs, the Pittsburgh Penguins donated Evgeni Malkin's jersey. It was important to them that we have it. Wearing that jersey, Malkin became the first Russian to win the Conn Smythe Trophy as the playoffs' Most Valuable Player.

However, to me, the best donations come from you, the fans. Without your generosity we simply could not be the foremost authority on hockey's history.

What I like most about receiving fan donations are the stories behind the artifacts — stories about the players, the teams and the leagues who used the items, as well as the circumstances surrounding how they arrived at the Hockey Hall of Fame. Those stories are often just as interesting as the artifacts themselves.

Recently, John MacMillan, who came up through the college ranks in the United States and had a lengthy professional career including two Stanley Cup victories with the Toronto Maple Leafs in the early 1960s, was traveling to Toronto to take part in the 50th anniversary celebrations for the

Leafs' 1962 Cup win. Prior to the trip he and his wife were reminiscing about John's early career and they happened to come across his old college hockey equipment; the next thing they did was call the Hockey Hall of Fame. We were honored and thrilled to get the call, and John was honored and thrilled that we were interested in his jerseys.

The Soviet National Team jersey worn by Vsevolod Bobrov at the 1954 World Championship (page 156) is one of my personal favorites in the book. Who would have thought that the "Big Red Machine" in Russia would have started off wearing bright blue? Another favorite is the trio of Boston Bruins jerseys worn by the famed Kraut Line (page 18). Those jerseys span three decades — from the 1930s to the 1950s — and the line, made up of Milt Schmidt, Woody Dumart and Bobby Bauer, played together their entire career; not only in the NHL, but in junior, minor-pro and even in the Royal Canadian Air Force. Amazing!

At the Hockey Hall of Fame we are fortunate to be able to see these artifacts every day, and it is our supreme pleasure to share them with you. As you flip through the pages of this book, enjoy the beautiful photographs that expertly capture the wide array of fabrics, colors, logos and crests, and immerse yourself in the stories behind each jersey. I know I will.

And remember, somewhere in those basements, attics or storage units might be that old Hamilton Tigers or Toronto St. Patricks jersey we have always been looking for. Or maybe it will be that unique sweater from the Western Hockey League that featured Johnny Canuck. Regardless of whether you call it a jersey or a sweater, we'll have a home for it at the Hockey Hall of Fame. We will preserve it, conserve it and have it on display for hockey fans around the world to see.

By the way, I call them hockey jerseys, and the best ones are game worn.

Enjoy!

Phil Pritchard
Vice President and Curator
Hockey Hall of Fame

NHL GREATS

The NHL is where the best in the world come to play. This collection — encompassing the jerseys of some of the NHL's most prominent players at various stages in their careers — exhibits fabrics and styles across generations and from professional, amateur and international competition.

Maurice "Rocket" Richard, whose legendary piercing eyes and steely resolve can be seen at right, wore this jersey while playing with the Montreal Canadiens in the 1950s. The latter half of the decade was a prodigious time for the Canadiens, as the club won five consecutive Stanley Cups (1955–56 to 1959–60).

RICHARD

1961

Maurice Richard

HE STARTED OUT WITH a different number and a different nickname than the ones he immortalized, but his eyes never, ever changed.

Even in his final seasons you could see the fire in his eyes: a flame that intensified as he approached the net.

"It was terrifying," goalie Glenn Hall has often said about the sight of Maurice "Rocket" Richard furiously bearing down on the net.

The Rocket's original nickname in the Montreal French press was "Le Comet," but it lacked staying power. When Montreal Canadiens' center Ray Getliffe remarked that Richard "went in like a rocket" toward the goal, a sports writer — the *Montreal Star's* Baz O'Meara and the *Montreal Gazette's* Dink Carroll are usually given credit — took that observation and made the nickname Richard's forever.

The Canadiens' Jacques Plante said it was the best moniker ever hung on an athlete, and not only because of the way Richard "would turn on the rockets" once he hit the blue line. Plante, who was the goalie when the Canadiens won the Stanley Cup in each of Richard's last five seasons, liked to quote "The Star-Spangled Banner" line —"the rocket's red glare" — in reference to Richard's burning eyes.

Richard, followed by Gordie Howe, made No. 9 the most important sweater number in hockey for at least two generations. But Richard started with No. 15 as a Canadiens rookie in 1942–43, and asked for the new number the next season because his first child, daughter Huguette, was born weighing exactly nine pounds. He scored 32 goals that season and another 12 in nine playoff games to lead the Canadiens to their first Stanley Cup in 13 years.

But it was between 1943–44 and 1944–45 that the legend of the Rocket really began to take root. In the opening round of the 1943–44 playoffs he scored all five Montreal goals in a Game 2 victory against the Toronto Maple Leafs. And it was that season that he joined with Hector "Toe" Blake and Elmer Lach to form the legendary Punch Line. The trio became the NHL's most formidable unit, combining for a then record 220 points in 1944–45. On December 28, 1944, Richard again had five goals (as well as three assists) in an evening game against the Detroit Red Wings despite being exhausted from moving his young family into a new home that day. Come the end of that 1944–45 season, Richard became the first NHL player to score 50 goals in a season, doing it in 50 games. Today, scoring 50 goals in the first 50 games of a season is the benchmark for superlative scoring prowess in the NHL.

Richard prevailed over several serious injuries, and his determination and tenacity allowed him to become the first NHLer to reach the 500-goal plateau. He played with anger and muscle, and his temper led him to strike an official, which in turn led to the famous 1955 suspension that cost him the chance at his only scoring title and barred him from playing throughout the entire playoffs. The suspension precipitated the infamous St. Patrick's Day riots, and Richard himself had to release a public plea to angered fans to stop rioting. His battles with league president Clarence Campbell are often cited as the true seeds of Quebec's Quiet Revolution.

He was so important to Quebec history and culture that at the official closing of the Montreal Forum in 1996, the crowd chanted his name for 16 emotional minutes; his state funeral in May 2000 was the first ever accorded to a Canadian athlete.

KENNEDY

1966

Ted Kennedy

L ONG AFTER HE HAD FINISHED playing, the trademark intonation — slow and almost mournful — still occasionally rose from the "greens" of Maple Leaf Gardens. "C'm-m-m-o-n-n-n, Teeder!"

Ted "Teeder" Kennedy was a star center for the Toronto Maple Leafs when they became the NHL's first dynasty, winning five Stanley Cups in the seven seasons from 1945 to 1951. More than a half-century after his retirement, Kennedy is still considered the quintessential Leaf and prototypical hockey captain: not necessarily the flashiest or highest-paid player or the best skater on the ice, but the most reliably consistent player who always rises to the occasion.

And he had his own distinctive sound track during his 14-year career — all spent with the Maple Leafs — which was just as important to Toronto's ambience as the clang of streetcars. Whenever the Leafs were desperate for a goal, Toronto fan John Arnott would bellow his famous drawl of "Come on Teeder!"

"Theodore" was Kennedy's given name, but Teeder was easier for his young friends to pronounce, and it stuck. The Montreal Canadiens brought him to training camp when he was just 16, but Kennedy, a lifelong Leafs fan, didn't like Montreal and came home to play in the prestigious Ontario Hockey Association Senior League instead. His Port Colborne Sailors' coach, Hockey Hall of Famer Nels Stewart, recommended Kennedy to the Leafs, and Conn Smythe reluctantly traded Frank Eddolls to the Canadiens for his rights.

The 18-year-old Kennedy joined the Leafs for the 1943–44 season and finished second on the team in scoring. When the Leafs upset the Canadiens in the 1945 Stanley Cup final, Kennedy led the Leafs with seven playoff goals and he, Bob Davidson and Mel Hill limited the impact of the Habs' famous Punch Line, which was 1-2-3 in NHL scoring, with Maurice Richard leading the way, scoring 50 goals in 50 games.

The postseason always brought out the finest in Kennedy, who scored the winning goal in the 1947 final over the Canadiens to make him the youngest player in history to score a Stanley Cup winner; he led all playoff scorers with 14 points in the Leafs' 1948 Cup victory. He took over as captain from the legendary Syl Apps for the 1948–49 season, and the Leafs became the first NHL team ever to win three Stanley Cups in succession. In 1951 they won again on Bill Barilko's famous overtime goal.

That was the Leafs' last championship for 11 years. Kennedy, who scored at least 25 goals in four of his first five seasons, became better known for his playmaking, tenacity and unparalleled faceoff skills. In his final full season he was awarded the Hart Trophy as the league's Most Valuable Player, joining first-ever winner Frank Nighbor as the only Hart winners — outside of goalies — who didn't finish in the top 10 in scoring.

Kennedy always said that replacing Apps as Toronto's captain was the proudest day of his life, so it's fitting that in 1993 Apps' No. 10 and Kennedy's No. 9 jerseys were the first Leafs' "honored sweaters" hoisted to the rafters of Maple Leaf Gardens.

Milt Schmidt (top left, circa late 1930s), Woody Dumart (top right, 1948–49) and Bobby Bauer (bottom) wore these jerseys while playing on the formidable Kraut Line (seen at right). Their last game together was on March 18, 1952, when Bauer came out of a five-year retirement to wear this jersey and skate with his old line-mates.

The Kraut Line

THEIR NICKNAME WOULD never pass a political correctness test today, but for a decade the "Kraut Line" rolled easily off the tongue of every hockey fan.

Milt Schmidt, Bobby Bauer and Woody Dumart were all of German descent, all from Kitchener, Ontario, and did almost everything together, including sharing a one-room apartment and heading to Europe to fight a war against the country of their ancestry.

Playing with the Kitchener Greenshirts, 16-year-old Schmidt led the Ontario Hockey Association junior series in 1934–35 with 20 goals; Dumart, then playing defense, was the league's leading point-getter; and Bauer rounded out the troop, collecting 18 points in 11 games played. The Boston Bruins had signed all three the previous year and before dispatching them to the Providence Reds, the club's farm team, at the start of the 1936–37 season, Art Ross united them as a forward line. They clicked instantly in Providence, and the Reds' head coach, Albert Leduc, named them the Sauerkraut Line to reflect their heritage. That was soon shortened to the Kraut Line.

By 1937–38 the line was together in Boston igniting fans with their offensive prowess. They scored 36 goals and 98 points in their first NHL year, and the following season the Bruins won the Stanley Cup for the first time in 10 seasons after leading the league by 16 points. Boston finished first four straight years and won the championship again in 1941 with the first-ever four-game sweep in a Cup final; it was the last time the Bruins would hoist the Cup until 1970, when Schmidt would be their general manager.

In 1939–40 Schmidt led the NHL with 52 points, while his wingers tied for second at 42 points each — the first time in history that line-mates finished 1-2-3 in the scoring race.

At 6-foot-1 Dumart was the line's checking presence, and he was skilled; by the time he retired he was the highest scoring left-winger in Bruins' history. Right-winger Bauer was only 5-foot-7, but he made the NHL's Second All-Star Team four times and won three Lady Byng Trophies. Standing at 6 feet, Schmidt was the youngest and most accomplished player of the trio of boyhood friends, winning the NHL scoring championship in 1940 and the Hart Trophy in 1951, to go along with three First All-Star Team berths.

All three traveled to Montreal during the 1941–42 season to enlist in the Royal Canadian Air Force. In their last game before departing for Europe they totaled 22 points in an 8–1 victory over the Montreal Canadiens, after which players from both teams hoisted the line-mates to their shoulders and carried them off the ice.

The Kraut Line never objected to their nickname, and when campaigns were held during the war years to rename them — the Buddy Line and the Kitchener Kids were among the candidates — none of the substitutes stuck.

The troika returned safely from World War II to play two more years together, but Bauer's retirement in the spring of 1947 ended The Kraut Line's brilliant run. Bauer did come out of retirement on a special one-day contract in March 1952 for a tribute game, earning a goal and an assist against the Chicago Black Hawks, while Schmidt recorded his 200th career goal.

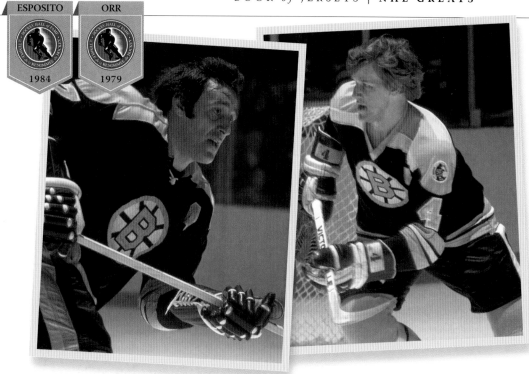

ESPOSITO 1984

ORR 1979

Phil Esposito (black) and Bobby Orr (white) wore these heavily repaired and tailored jerseys (notice the numerous repairs to Esposito's jersey and the sleeve alterations made to Orr's) during the Bruins heydays of the early 1970s. Both Bruins can be seen at left during this same time period.

Beantown's Best

FOR DECADES IT HAS BEEN the ideal blueprint: Build from within, then trade to complete assembly. But it has rarely been followed as perfectly as it was by the Big Bad Boston Bruins.

Of course — no matter how solid the foundation or good the construction — rarely do teams come away with as solid a one-two combination as Bobby Orr and Phil Esposito.

Orr arrived in Boston via the classic scouting and development intrigue that prevailed before the 1967 NHL expansion, and Esposito came to The Hub in one of the most lopsided trades in league history.

Esposito, who had already registered three 20-goal campaigns in his first four NHL seasons, was traded to Boston from the Chicago Black Hawks on May 15, 1967, along with Ken Hodge and Fred Stanfield, for Hubert "Pit" Martin, Jack Norris and Gilles Marotte. Hodge and Esposito would join with Bruins incumbent Wayne Cashman to form the dominant line of the first half of the 1970s.

Orr had been discovered in Parry Sound, Ontario, and to curry favor with him, the Bruins sponsored Orr's minor hockey team. In 1962, at the age of 14, Orr signed on with the Bruins organization and the club allowed him to commute to play games with the Ontario Hockey League's Oshawa Generals without ever practicing with the team. The Bruins then bought the Generals, even though they already owned a team in the same league in Niagara Falls.

Heading into the 1967–68 season, the first year Orr and Esposito joined forces, the Bruins had missed the playoffs eight years in a row, hadn't won the Stanley Cup since 1941 and, in a six-team league, had won only six NHL individual trophies over a 25-year span: two Lady Byng Trophies, two Calder Trophies and two Hart Trophies.

But by the end of 1974–75, the duo's last full season together, the Bruins of the Orr-Esposito era had amassed five Hart Memorial Trophies (three by Orr, two by Esposito), seven Art Ross Trophies (five by Esposito, two by Orr), eight James Norris Memorial Trophies (Orr), two Conn Smythe Trophies (Orr), a Calder Memorial Trophy (Orr), a Lady Byng Memorial Trophy (Johnny Bucyk) and two Stanley Cups.

Among hockey's most recognizable photos is the 1970 photograph of Orr in mid-flight after being tripped by St. Louis Blues defenseman Noel Picard just after scoring the overtime goal that gave the Bruins their first Stanley Cup in 39 years. It inspired the bronze statue now outside the Bruins' home arena. Earlier that year Orr became the first defenseman to lead the NHL in scoring and the first player at any position to record 100 assists in one season.

The Bruins' second Stanley Cup came in 1972 when Esposito and Orr finished 1–2 in scoring, while Orr won the Hart, Norris and Smythe Trophies and scored his second Stanley Cup–winning goal. In September that year, Esposito was the unchallenged spokesman and spiritual leader of Team Canada in the Summit Series.

In the season between those two championships, Ken Dryden's Montreal Canadiens upset the Bruins, but Esposito became the first NHLer to record 150 points and shattered the single-season goal-scoring record of 58 when he registered 76 tallies. Orr also established a new league record with his plus-124 rating and he set the points record for defensemen with 139.

Esposito established the template for the big center who owned the slot, while Orr's fleet end-to-end rushes, passing eye and puck-possession skills, all from the blue line, changed the game forever.

And together, they changed the destiny of the Boston Bruins.

LEETCH
2009

◄ **Brian Leetch (seen at right with the New York Rangers) wore this Cheshire High School Rams jersey for two seasons (1982–83, 1983–84) while leading his school to the Connecticut State championship in 1983–84. That season he recorded 52 goals and 101 points and was named an All-State defenseman.**

Brian Leetch

H E HAD FAVORITE PLAYERS, but he didn't have any role models, so Brian Leetch became one.

"I grew up in Connecticut, and no one was going to the NHL from there," recalls Leetch, the exception to the rule. "There was no one to show us the way. I didn't have a thought of the NHL when I was playing town hockey and high school. It was a far-off dream ... The only thing that seemed realistic was maybe the Olympics."

Four years after wearing this sweater for his hometown Cheshire High School Rams between 1982 and 1984, Leetch had not only played in the Olympics but in the NHL, too, kicking off an 18-year Hockey Hall of Fame career that included winning two James Norris Memorial Trophies and helping put an end to the NHL's longest Stanley Cup drought.

The Leetch family moved to Cheshire, Connecticut, when Brian was 5 years old because his father, Jack, had been hired to manage the new, privately owned Cheshire Skating Center.

Leetch grew up playing hockey and little league baseball; in fact, he developed such a hard fastball that he pitched the baseball Rams to a state title and later set the Avon Old Farms School record with 19 strikeouts in a game. But it was hockey that piqued his interest the most, even though he was nearly high-school age before professional hockey was televised in his area.

Leetch suited up for the Cheshire Rams for his freshman and sophomore years. His 1983–84 sophomore season was one for the ages: 52 goals and 101 points in just 28 games while earning honors as an All-State defenseman and leading the Rams to a state championship.

But heading into his junior season the skating center was sold and converted into a warehouse. With no town rink, Leetch transferred to Avon Old Farms School, an all-boys prep school in Avon, Connecticut, about a 20-minute drive from Cheshire.

Playing defense over his two seasons at Avon Old Farms, Leetch had a stunning offensive output of 70 goals and 90 assists in just 54 games. During this formative time Leetch met Hartford Whalers star Ron Francis, who encouraged him to keep working at his NHL dreams. Two decades later, Leetch and Francis were roommates while playing with the Toronto Maple Leafs.

Drafted ninth overall by the New York Rangers in 1986, Leetch enrolled at Boston College where, like his father before him, he became an All-Star defenseman. After a year in Boston and another with the United States Olympic team — with whom he skated in the 1988 Calgary Olympics — Leetch joined the Rangers and got off to a prophetic start, notching an assist in his first game: a February 29, 1988, contest against the St. Louis Blues that New York won 5–2.

In 1988–89, which was his official rookie season after having only played 17 games in 1987–88, he scored 23 goals, a record for rookie defensemen, and won the Calder Memorial Trophy. In his brilliant 16 seasons with the Rangers, he became the first American defenseman with a 100-point season and the first American to win the Conn Smythe Trophy, which he earned when the Rangers won the 1994 Stanley Cup, their first in 54 years.

Mark Messier called Leetch "the greatest Ranger of all time," and it's safe to say he is also the greatest hockey player to ever come out of Connecticut.

Wayne Gretzky, pictured at left ▶
with the Los Angeles Kings,
became hockey's biggest star
and helped grow the game in the
American south. He got his start
in Brantford, Ontario, with the
local Nadrofsky Steelers. He made
national headlines by the time he
was 10 years old and now holds
or shares 61 NHL records.

Wayne Gretzky

EVEN THE TALLEST TREE in the forest was once a sapling.

Wayne Gretzky — who grew into "The Great One," established 61 separate NHL records, won eight straight Hart Memorial Trophies and put the game on his back and carried it into several sun-belt markets — had to start somewhere. And that somewhere was the Brantford Minor Hockey Association.

When Gretzky started playing organized hockey as a 6-year-old in 1967 he was four years younger than many of his teammates and opponents because the atom level (typically for kids 10 years of age) was the lowest age classification in Brantford hockey. The standard-issue atom sweater was far too big for a player Gretzky's age, so to gain greater freedom of movement he began tucking the right side of his sweater into his hockey pants. It was a habit he maintained throughout his extraordinary 20-year career in the NHL and it became one of the enduring symbols of his inimitable style.

Gretzky could already skate well by the time he suited up as an under-ager for atom hockey. In fact, he'd taken his first steps on ice at a pond on his paternal grandparents' cucumber farm when he was still two months shy of his third birthday.

His famous father, Walter Gretzky, eventually grew tired of "freezing while I waited for him to play hockey all day in the park" and built a rink in the flat backyard of the family's Varadi Avenue home. Wayne, his sister and three brothers could play there as long as they wanted, and when Walter wasn't putting them through drills skating around

bottles, he could supervise from the warmth of his home. That rink became known as the Wally Coliseum, and once Wayne began lighting up the NHL it spawned an entire cottage industry in Canada.

Gretzky, who originally wore No. 3, had only one goal in his first year, but he began scoring in unprecedented bunches soon after. He transferred to No. 9 as he got older — an homage to his idol, Gordie Howe — and gained national attention for the first time with Brantford's Nadrofsky Steelers. In his breakout year as an 8-year-old he wore the sweater shown here and recorded 167 points. As a 10-year-old, he toppled that number with 378 goals and 139 assists for 517 points and was nicknamed "The White Tornado" (after the Ajax brand of cleaner and its slogan of the day) because of the white gloves he wore.

After two years of Junior A with Toronto's Seneca Nationals, Gretzky played his only year of major junior hockey with the Ontario Hockey League's Sault Ste. Marie Greyhounds at the age of 16 in 1977–78. He finished second in league scoring while also settling on the No. 99 that he would make famous and, ultimately, inaccessible in the NHL (since his retirement the NHL retired No. 99 league wide). It was team veteran Brian Gualazzi who had squatter's rights on No. 9, forcing Gretzky to choose a new number.

Gretzky, like Muhammad Ali, Michael Jordan and Babe Ruth, came to transcend his sport, and while he started off as a No. 3 in Brantford, he made No. 99 a symbol for excellence worldwide. Perhaps it was no accident that No. 99 retired in 1999 and was inducted into the Hall of Fame that same year. The date of that induction, November 22, also happened to be the same date of the informal founding of the NHL.

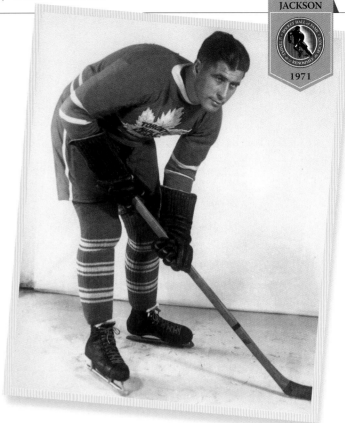

◄ The New York Americans, sometimes called the "Star Spangled Skaters" for their red, white and blue star-adorned attire, lasted 17 seasons in the NHL (1926–27 to 1941–42). Busher Jackson wore this jersey for his two seasons with the club, 1939–40 and 1940–41. He is shown at right early in his career with the Toronto Maple Leafs.

Busher Jackson

BY THE LATE 1930s, the New York Americans were no longer first in the hearts and minds of the New York hockey fans who patronized Madison Square Garden.

The Americans, a financially sinking ship, were doing whatever they could to attract more customers and to help pay the rent after years of playing second fiddle to the New York Rangers, the team owned by the Madison Square Garden proprietors.

The Americans had loaded their lineup with veteran players, hoping they would lead the team into the playoffs — which would in turn win them support — after only making it to the postseason twice in their first 12 years of existence. The veterans panned out and the Americans made the playoffs for three straight seasons from 1937–38 to 1939–40, but the Rangers countered by winning the 1940 Stanley Cup, negating the efforts of their co-tenants.

The Americans, who had already reunited two-thirds of the Montreal Maroons notorious S Line by signing both Nels Stewart and Reginald "Hooley" Smith, also reunited two-thirds of the legendary Kid Line when they signed both Charlie Conacher and Harvey "Busher" Jackson for the start of the 1939–40 season.

Jackson started in the NHL with the Toronto Maple Leafs during the 1929–30 season, after having spent the previous two seasons playing for the Toronto Marlboros, the Leafs' development team. Conacher had joined the Leafs from the Marlboros as well, and two days before New Year's Eve 1929, Jackson, Conacher and Joe Primeau had been united on what became known as the Kid Line — the most celebrated troika in Toronto hockey history.

At just 18 years old, Jackson was confident to the point of brashness, and he earned his nickname when trainer Tim Daly, responding to Jackson's refusal to do the rookies' duty of stick-carrying, called him "nothing but a fresh busher."

But Jackson had already proven he was no bush-leaguer: In his first NHL game, three months shy of his 19th birthday, he decked Montreal Canadiens superstar Howie Morenz.

An infectious personality, Jackson brought a swashbuckling flair to the left side of the Kid Line. Big and talented, with a strong shot both forehand and backhand, he succeeded Morenz as the NHL scoring champion in 1932 when he was just 21 years old. (Jackson stood as the youngest scoring champ until Wayne Gretzky won his first Art Ross Trophy at the age of 20.)

After Jackson finished second in scoring in 1933, Conacher won two straight scoring titles. When Gordie Drillon — who had become Jackson's line-mate by then — won in 1938, it made four Toronto scoring champions in seven years, the greatest stretch in franchise history. No Toronto player has won a scoring title since.

When Jackson's production waned a bit, the Leafs sent him to the Americans. He played two seasons in New York, registering 20 and 26 points. After an early playoff exit in 1939–40 and missing the playoffs altogether in 1940–41, Jackson finished his career with three years with the Boston Bruins, where his point totals rebounded and he even spent some time on defense.

After the 1941–42 season, as the United States entered World War II, the New York Americans suspended operations. They planned to return, but never did, and New York City was a one-team hockey town until the New York Islanders arrived in 1972.

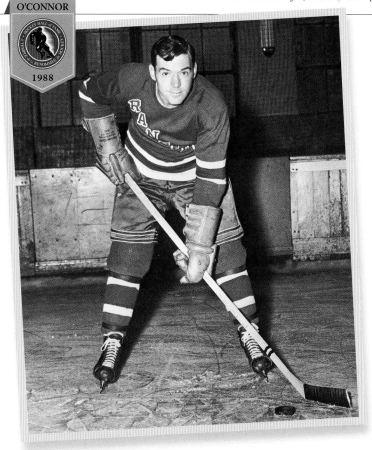

O'CONNOR

1988

Buddy O'Connor, shown at left in his first years with the New York Rangers, likely wore this jersey for his first season with the club in 1947–48, where he won both the Hart and Lady Byng trophies and was named Canada's athlete of the year (1948). ▶

Buddy O'Connor

HERBERT "BUDDY" O'CONNOR'S hockey acumen was honed in Montreal, but it was in New York City that he accomplished something the hockey world had never seen before.

In 1947–48, his first season with the New York Rangers after spending the first 16 years of his career playing junior, senior and NHL hockey in Montreal, O'Connor won both the Hart Trophy and the Lady Byng Trophy. It was the first time that any player had captured both pieces of hardware in the same season. And only four players since then have been able to balance the aggression required to be the league's Most Valuable Player and the sportsmanship needed to be named its most gentlemanly player.

Not only was O'Connor the first NHLer to win both the Hart and Lady Byng trophies, he was the first New York Ranger ever to be named league MVP. Over their first 68 years in the league, the Broadway Blueshirts won the most prestigious individual award just three times: O'Connor in 1948, Chuck Rayner two years later and Andy Bathgate in 1959. Mark Messier in 1992 is the only other Ranger to claim the Hart Trophy.

Had O'Connor scored just two more points in 1947–48, he would have been a triple-trophy winner. As it was, the Montreal Canadiens' Elmer Lach edged him by a single point for the scoring title.

At just 142 pounds, O'Connor was one of the lightest players in the NHL, but he made a heavy impact in the four years he spent in

a Rangers sweater. The 60 points and 24 goals he scored in his double-trophy year were both career highs, but to the fans who packed Madison Square Garden his most important influence that year was in the standings. Before O'Connor's arrival for the 1947–48 season, the Rangers had last made the playoffs in 1941–42 — a drought of five straight years since last tasting postseason action. O'Connor put the Rangers back in the playoffs during his first year. Two years later, with O'Connor as captain, the club made it all the way to the seventh game of the Stanley Cup final before losing a heartbreaker to the Detroit Red Wings in double overtime. It would be another 22 seasons before the Rangers advanced that deep into the playoffs again.

Originally told by the Montreal Junior Royals that he was too small, O'Connor went on to star for both the junior and senior Royals, winning a Quebec Senior scoring title. With World War II thinning the Montreal Canadiens roster, the entire Razzle Dazzle Line — O'Connor between his boyhood friend Pete Morin and Gerry Heffernan — was promoted from the Royals to the Canadiens. O'Connor won two Stanley Cups in six years with the Canadiens, but in 1947 they dealt him to the Rangers, apparently thinking that at 31 he was too old to be effective.

Two major trophies — and almost three — proved them dead wrong.

O'Connor was the first of 11 men originally elected to the Hockey Hall of Fame in the special "Veteran Category," which was established in 1988 and abandoned in 2000 when the 11 were placed in the regular players' category.

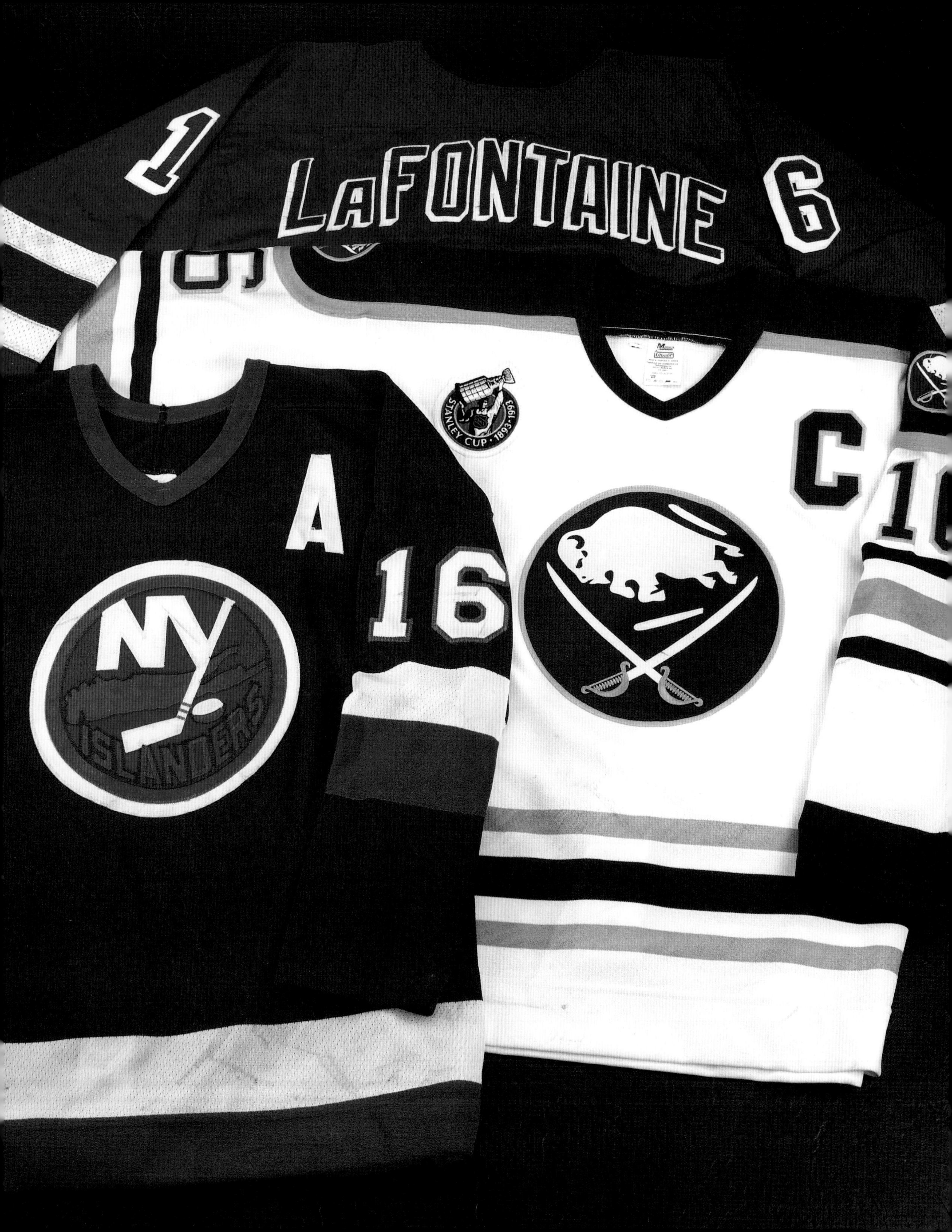
LaFONTAINE 6
A
16
NY
ISLANDERS
STANLEY CUP · 1893-1993
C

◄ Brett Hull wore this jersey during the 1989–90 season, the campaign he joined his famous father, Bobby, as a 50-goal scorer. Brett finished with a league-leading 72 goals and earned a berth on the First All-Star Team as well as the Lady Byng Memorial Trophy as the league's most gentlemanly player. Brett is shown at right during the 1992–93 season.

Brett Hull

WITH HEREDITY ON HIS SIDE, Brett Hull was born to score goals — and he did it everywhere he stopped on his road to the Hockey Hall of Fame.

But nowhere did "The Golden Brett" do it with such emphasis, and while engendering such gratitude, as he did in St. Louis during the early 1990s.

The Calgary Flames, who had shuttled Hull between the minors and the NHL over his first two seasons, traded the 23-year-old to the St. Louis Blues in March of 1988. The Flames had drafted him 117th overall two years earlier and clearly did not project him as one of the top three goal-scorers in NHL history. But that is exactly what Bobby "The Golden Jet" Hull's son became.

He wore sweater No. 16 with St. Louis — the same number his famous father wore during his first four seasons with the Chicago Black Hawks — and made it synonymous with the Hull name once again.

In his first full season with the Blues — and in the NHL for that matter — Hull scored 41 goals and won the Lady Byng Memorial Trophy. The next fall, center Adam Oates arrived in St. Louis from the Detroit Red Wings, and the prolific pair was tagged "Hull and Oates" after the best-selling musical duo Hall and Oates. Oates' creativity in getting Hull the puck resulted in The Golden Brett notching 72 goals, making him the first player to record 50 or more goal seasons in the National Collegiate Athletic Association (52 with the University of Minnesota-Duluth in 1986), the American Hockey League (50 with the Moncton Golden Flames in 1987) and the NHL.

In 1990–91 Oates had 90 assists and Hull scored 86 goals, the third-highest total ever recorded and the single-season record for goals by a right-winger. He won the Hart Memorial Trophy as the league's Most Valuable Player, and his 131 points set a Blues franchise record that still stands. That fall he led Team USA in scoring during their run to the Canada Cup silver medal.

Even though Oates was traded late in the 1991–92 season, Hull still scored 70 times. It was his third straight season with 70 goals or more, and the second straight year that he scored his first 50 goals within his first 50 games, making him the only player other than Wayne Gretzky to do so in back-to-back years. Hull followed his 70-goal season with 54 goals in 1992–93 and 57 goals in 1993–94, running his string of 50-plus-goal seasons to five in a row.

In Hull's 11 seasons in St. Louis, the Blues never advanced past the conference semifinals, and in 1998–99 he signed with the Dallas Stars, where because No. 16 was already taken he wore No. 22 for one year. Hull's highly controversial goal against the Buffalo Sabres' Dominik Hasek in the third overtime of Game 6 of the 1998–99 Stanley Cup final gave the Stars their first Stanley Cup championship. He won the Cup again with the Detroit Red Wings in 2002 when he and Hasek were teammates and roommates on the road.

Hull signed with the Phoenix Coyotes — formerly the Winnipeg Jets — just prior to the NHL lockout, and they reactivated his father's No. 9 jersey from retirement especially for him. When play resumed in the fall of 2005 Hull played only five games before retiring.

A year later the St. Louis Blues retired his number and renamed the street in front of their arena Brett Hull Way, with the rink address scheduled to become No. 16.

BARRY

1965

Marty Barry, shown at left wearing the winged wheel, wore this Detroit Red Wings jersey during one of his four seasons with the club (1935–36 to 1938–39). In 1942, the retired Barry wore this All-Star jersey in the "Victory All-Star Game." On a team of retired NHLers, Barry played against the Boston Bruins to raise funds for U.S. Army Relief.

Marty Barry

MARTY BARRY MAY be among the lesser-known Hockey Hall of Fame inductees, but, as this pair of sweaters donated by his family illustrates, he was always on the vanguard of history.

A technically skilled iron man who missed only two games in his first 10 NHL seasons, Barry finished among the NHL's top five scorers five times, and tied with Harvey "Busher" Jackson for most points in the 1930s.

He scored the winning goal in the Detroit Red Wings' first Stanley Cup victory, played in the longest game in NHL history, led all playoff scorers in 1937, and played in two of the invitational matches that set the stage for the NHL's official All-Star Game.

"He was with the Bruins, who led the league in 1934–35, but didn't win the Cup," Barry's daughter Barbara Cormier says. "So the Bruins manager, Art Ross, really wanted to get Cooney Weiland. He and Jack Adams [manager] of the Red Wings were talking, and Adams said he could have Weiland if the Bruins gave Dad to the Red Wings. That's how the deal was made, just talking. And Adams said later, 'Art Ross just gave me the Stanley Cup.'

"And they did win it that year, for the first time," Cormier says. "And they won it again the next year too."

That made the Red Wings the first American-based team to win back-to-back Stanley Cups. Centering a potent line, with Herbie Lewis and Larry Aurie on the flanks, Barry wore No. 7 on his Red Wings sweater, which was his from 1935 to 1939, before he played one final NHL season, this time lacing up with the Montreal Canadiens.

The first benefit game Barry played was the 1937 Howie Morenz Memorial Game, which took place in Montreal to raise money for the deceased superstar's family.

In 1942, two years after he had retired from the NHL, Barry played in a fund-raising invitational at Boston Garden on an off night for both the NHL and the American Hockey League. A group of retired NHL All-Stars — including George "Red" Horner and Eddie Shore (who played in every major benefit game) — tied the Bruins 4–4 in a non-bodychecking game of two 15-minute periods. The game was played before a regularly scheduled Eastern Amateur League match between the Johnston Bluebirds and Boston Olympics.

The "Victory All-Star Game," as it was called, was played just three months after Pearl Harbor and raised funds for U.S. Army Relief. It also helped create an appetite for the NHL's inaugural All-Star Game, which debuted in 1947.

When Cormier and her husband, Paul, received the sweaters from her mother, they luckily came wrapped in plastic bags, because they sat in a closet in the Cormier home for a number of years.

"It was amazing that they were not eaten by moths," she says. "You see so many of the other sweaters with lots of holes in them, but these were in great shape."

The family made the final decision, as a group, to donate Barry's sweaters to the Hockey Hall of Fame in 1998, although they were being pressured by other museums and collectors to sell for a profit.

"Someone in the family said, 'I wonder what Dad would have wanted,'" Cormier recalls. "And then it was unanimous."

Longtime Toronto Maple Leafs captain George Armstrong wore this jersey throughout the 1966–67 season and playoffs. Armstrong, shown at right celebrating a Stanley Cup victory in 1963, led the Leafs to their fourth Stanley Cup of the decade by scoring the empty net Cup-clinching goal over the Montreal Canadiens on May 2, 1967.

George Armstrong

GEORGE ARMSTRONG CERTAINLY knows what it takes to win. Wherever he skated for the Toronto Maple Leafs organization, a major trophy seemed to join him. Nicknamed "The Chief" in recognition of his Iroquois heritage, Armstrong hoisted the Stanley Cup four times while wearing the "C" on the upper left side of his Toronto Maple Leafs sweater. He also won the Allan Cup playing for the Leafs' senior Marlboros farm team in 1950; won the American Hockey League championship playing for the Pittsburgh Hornets (Toronto's professional farm team) in 1951; and after retiring coached the Toronto Marlies (Toronto's junior farm club) to both the 1973 and 1975 Memorial Cup.

In the 1966–67 season, when Armstrong wore this sweater, his aging and underdog Leafs went on to defeat the archrival Montreal Canadiens four games to two for their fourth Stanley Cup of the 1960s and the franchise's 13th overall. And much to Armstrong's continuing surprise, no other Leaf captain has held the Cup aloft since then.

"You had absolutely no idea that it wouldn't happen again quickly," he says. "I never thought it would be this long, but I sense it could be happening again soon."

Armstrong scored the final goal of the Original Six era into an empty net to cement the Leafs' 3–1 victory over the Canadiens in the Cup-clinching game at Maple Leaf Gardens. Another future Hockey Hall of Famer, Bob Pulford, got the puck up to Armstrong as he was about to hit center ice.

"I remember going down the right side, and Montreal's Ralph Backstrom was coming across, not to get me, but to block my shot," says Armstrong. "I waited until the last second so he wouldn't get in the way of the shot. I could have shot earlier."

It was historically appropriate that the only two Canadian teams of the time would meet in the last Stanley Cup final before the NHL expanded. It was the country's massively celebrated centennial year, and Montreal itself was just opening Expo 67, one of the most successful World Fairs ever. Five months later, the value of Canada's gift to the world would be confirmed by the doubling of the NHL into 12 teams — the new clubs expanding into important American markets.

More than four decades later, 1967 is still the Leafs' last playoff victory over Montreal. They've met only twice since then, with the Habs sweeping both series.

Armstrong, a diligent player who personified the Leafs' workmanlike ethic, signed a "C-card" contract with the Leafs in 1947, when he was 16. He went on to serve as captain for 11 seasons, the longest such tenure in Leafs history. After a nine-year stint as a scout for the Quebec Nordiques (1978 to 1987), he returned to scout for the Leafs and is still with the club — 65 years after his first contract.

"I turned down signing with the Bruins," he says of his early days. "Ever since I was a little kid I wanted to play for the Leafs, probably from hearing them on the radio with Foster Hewitt. I've become a member for life."

PULFORD

1991

Bob Pulford (shown at left in his final days with the Toronto Maple Leafs) wore this gold and purple Los Angeles Kings jersey – royal colors also used by the Los Angeles Lakers (both franchises were owned by Jack Kent Cooke) – for his final NHL season. Upon retirement Pulford took over coaching duties for the Kings. ▶

Bob Pulford

HAD HE NOT ALREADY QUALIFIED as a player, Bob Pulford could make a good case for enshrinement to the Hockey Hall of Fame as a builder.

After playing his final two NHL seasons with the Los Angeles Kings, Pulford stepped behind the bench and helped the team regain admittance to the playoffs, as well as regain the respect of their fans. He then moved on to Chicago, where whether he acted as coach, general manager or vice president of the team, the Chicago Black Hawks made the playoffs for 21 straight years.

But before all that, Pulford was a strong two-way center and a core player on two Memorial Cup and four Stanley Cup championship teams.

After leading the Toronto Maple Leafs–owned Toronto Marlboros to the 1955 and 1956 national junior titles, Pulford graduated to the parent Maple Leafs, who were in a deep trough and rebuilding from the star-studded dynasty of the late 1940s. In Pulford's rookie season, the young Leafs missed the playoffs and they fell short again the following season. But then the pieces, including Pulford, came together, and Toronto made the playoffs every season until the NHL's first year of expansion, winning Stanley Cups in 1962, 1963, 1964 and 1967, the latter coming when most of the Leafs, including Pulford, were considered well beyond their primes.

In an era when scoring 20 goals was a major plateau, Pulford was good for an almost-automatic 18-plus goals per year, and he registered 20 or more goals four times in his 14 years with the Leafs. But he was also assigned to cover the opposition's best line, and Gordie Howe once described Pulford as one of his "private headaches." A team with less pure star power than the Montreal Canadiens, Detroit Red Wings or Chicago Black Hawks, the Leafs still tied the Habs for the most Stanley Cups of the 1960s, and Montreal coach Hector "Toe" Blake always said that Pulford was the "heart and soul of their team."

A strong leader, Pulford was an alternate captain of the Leafs until he helped former schoolmate Alan Eagleson form the National Hockey League Players' Association. Leafs owner Conn Smythe was angered and stripped Pulford of his "A," but Pulford still became the association's first president.

Pulford was traded to the Kings just before the 1970–71 season and he encountered a Los Angeles hockey scene that, although new, was already in decline. The Kings were in the throes of a four-year playoff drought that would not end until 1973–74, Pulford's second year as coach. He played two years with the Kings, the second as captain, before going behind the bench.

To match their nickname, the Kings were dressed in regal purple and gold, just like the NBA's Los Angeles Lakers — both franchises just happened to be owned by the same man, Canadian Jack Kent Cooke. The Kings played out of Cooke's brand-new arena, nicknamed the "Fabulous Forum," which he built because the Western Hockey League's Los Angeles Blades were the preferred tenant at the Los Angeles Memorial Sports Arena. Cooke once complained and explained his team's lackluster attendance numbers by insinuating that the 500,000 Canadians who called southern California home did so because they all hated hockey.

But when Pulford became coach — and Rogie Vachon arrived to play net — the Kings made the playoffs for nine straight years, and the NHL got a toehold in its first sustainable warm-weather market.

◀ **Defenseman Harry Howell (shown at right with the New York Rangers) wore this New York Golden Blades jersey during the first portion of the 1973–74 World Hockey Association season. Midway through the campaign, the Blades moved to New Jersey and became the Knights.**

Harry Howell

HARRY HOWELL WORE a New York Rangers sweater for 1,160 games, more than any other player in franchise history, but it was in another New York sweater — worn for less than half a season — that he had some of the most colorful times of his exemplary career.

Howell played in the NHL for 22 years, the first 17 for the Rangers before splitting time between the Oakland Seals and the Los Angeles Kings. Then in 1973 he signed with the World Hockey Association's New York Golden Blades. The WHA had debuted the previous year and had planned on establishing New York as one of its power bases. The then-named New York Raiders had trouble drawing crowds at Madison Square Garden and were repossessed by the league. The team was sold to Ralph Brent for the 1973–74 season. Brent renamed the club the Golden Blades and, like the logo (seen at left), he ordered the players to wear white skates.

"The guys all hated that, they looked like figure skates," recalls Howell, the team captain and eventual player-coach.

"It was just wild playing for that team," Howell says. "We always got paid, which not everyone in that league did, but our owner never came to the games. For the games we played in New York, the players had to stand in line for their checks. While they were waiting, I'd go down to the box office and they'd give me money from the receipts from that very night's game. Then I'd pay the players."

Needless to say, the situation couldn't last for long. By late November, the league had taken the team over again and moved it to the suburb of Cherry Hill, New Jersey, where the club was given its third name in 18 months: the New Jersey Knights.

Things weren't much better in Jersey than they were in Manhattan: the rink had a serious slope and there was only one useable dressing room.

"We had that dressing room, and the visiting team had to dress in the hotel and wear their uniforms to the game," Howell chuckles, "just like in peewee house league."

At the end of the year, the franchise moved yet again, becoming the San Diego Mariners. Howell went to San Diego with the team, played a year there and the next year moved to the WHA's Calgary Cowboys before retiring partway through the season. He returned in 1974–75 to coach the Mariners and later became general manager of the NHL's Cleveland Barons before becoming coach of the NHL's Minnesota North Stars.

When he retired, Howell had dressed for more games on defense — 1,411 in the NHL, 170 in the WHA — than any other player in professional hockey history. Although he never won the Stanley Cup as a player, he was awarded the James Norris Memorial Trophy as the NHL's top defenseman in 1967, his 15th season.

"I said when I won 'It's a good thing I got it now because that kid in Boston [Bobby Orr] is going to win the next six or seven,'" Howell laughs. "But I underestimated. Bobby won the next eight."

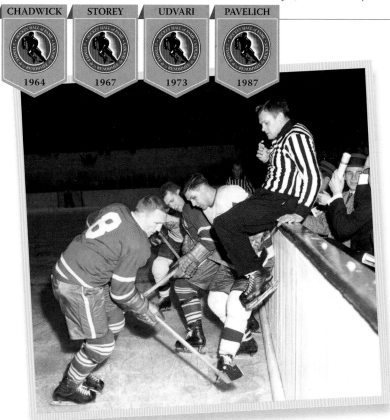

CHADWICK	STOREY	UDVARI	PAVELICH
1964	1967	1973	1987

Five officials jerseys spanning the 1940s to the 1970s and illustrating all manner of designs, including: stripes, colors, collars, arm bands, name plates and numbers. From top to bottom, left to right: Matt Pavelich (circa 1970s), Bill Chadwick (circa 1940s), Gregg Madill (1979 World Championship), Red Storey (circa 1950s) and Frank Udvari (circa 1950s) – who can be seen at left avoiding the play.

Whistle Blowers

BEING THE COMPETITIVE and volatile game that it is, hockey could never have grown so big without them. Referees and linesmen are supposed to be at their best when they go unnoticed, but the NHL has had some of the most memorable officials in all of professional sport. For much of the game's history, committed fans have been as familiar with the styles and attitudes of individual officials, particularly referees, as with those of players.

They are often mocked as zebras — although that term only became relevant after 1955, when NHL officials wore striped sweaters for the first time — and regularly called blind; and at least one of them partially was.

Bill Chadwick, the first legendary referee from the United States, was blinded in one eye while trying out for the U.S. National Team and soon turned to officiating. He hid his impairment for his entire officiating career, which included 15 seasons and over 900 regular-season games in the NHL, as well as a record 42 Stanley Cup–final games. Chadwick individually pioneered the referee's hand signals during the 1940s, and the league formally adopted his system in 1956, one year after he retired.

Chadwick's V-neck official sweater from the 1940s was fashioned from very fine white wool. It is casual and stylish, not unlike a sweater a collegian of the era would wear.

Not so chic was the orange sweater Frank Udvari wore when he began his NHL refereeing career in 1952. Considered one of the best referees of all time, Udvari missed only two games in his 15-year career and he officiated the game that led to the famous 1955 Montreal riots: he gave Maurice Richard a match penalty, resulting in the Rocket's season-ending suspension. Twelve years after Udvari retired he was forced back into action when referee Dave Newell was injured. Acting as NHL supervisor at a New York Islanders–Atlanta Flames game, he borrowed a pair of skates from the Islanders' Bryan Trottier, then disallowed a Trottier goal late in the game. Udvari later donated the skates to the Hockey Hall of Fame.

That tale could have been part of the repertoire of the game's great "storey" teller. Roy "Red" Storey, who once scored three touchdowns in the Grey Cup for the Toronto Argonauts, was talkative and funny, but principled. He worked every Stanley Cup final from 1953 to 1958, and the players loved him. But when league president Clarence Campbell publicly criticized his work in a 1959 semifinal game, he immediately quit and never returned to the NHL.

While the NHL referees were always considered the best in the world, none had ever refereed at a world championship until pressure from Canada put Gregg Madill into this International Ice Hockey Federation sweater for the 1979 Worlds in Moscow. Madill officiated the Worlds without much hullabaloo, but he did make waves in the NHL that year when he was the on-ice official for the infamous Boston–New York postgame brawl that saw members of the Boston Bruins fighting the fans.

When the Hockey Hall of Fame decided to recognize linesmen in 1987, Matt Pavelich was the first inductee. In 1955, he and his older brother Marty, of the Detroit Red Wings, became the first official-player combination in the same game. His 31 years included 1,727 games, second behind Neil Armstrong, and only John D'Amico lined more playoff games than Pavelich's 245.

Paul
Stewart
#22
1000
31/15/03

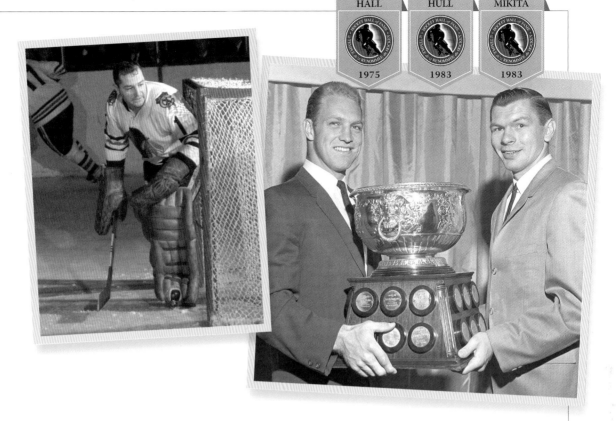

HALL	HULL	MIKITA
1975	1983	1983

Franchise saviors center Stan Mikita (top jersey, circa 1970), goalie Glenn Hall (middle jersey, circa 1958) and left-winger Bobby Hull (bottom jersey, 1969) transformed the Chicago Black Hawks from a middling squad to a fierce contender, leading the club to its first Stanley Cup in 23 years in 1961. Hull and Mikita are seen at right holding the Art Ross Trophy, while Hall is shown in net.

Windy City Greats

THEY HAD LOTS OF HELP from an excellent supporting cast, but it was this trio of headliners who prompted one of the most dramatic franchise reversals in NHL history.

In the dozen seasons between the fall of 1946 and the spring of 1958, the Chicago Black Hawks (their name was officially changed to Blackhawks in 1986) made the playoffs just twice and never advanced past the opening round.

But just before the last season of that futile stretch, the Hawks obtained goaltender Glenn Hall from the Detroit Red Wings and promoted left-winger Bobby Hull from the St. Catharines Teepees, their junior affiliate. When slick center Stan Mikita arrived from the Teepees two years later, the core of a dynamic new era in Chicago hockey was in place.

No longer doormats, the Hawks missed the playoffs just once in the next 40 years. In 1961 they won their first Stanley Cup in 23 years, with Hall, Hull and Mikita all playing critical roles, along with fellow future Hockey Hall of Famer, defenseman Pierre Pilote. Mikita was the leading playoff goal scorer; Hull had 14 points in the Hawks' 12 playoff games; and Hall was simply brilliant, recording two shutouts and the lowest playoff goals-against average (2.02) of his career.

The Black Hawks didn't win any individual trophies or place anyone on the NHL's First All-Star Team that year, but over their Chicago careers, Hall, Hull and Mikita all produced a bumper crop of accolades.

Hall won two of his three Vezina Trophies with the Hawks (1963

and 1967), and in his 10 Chicago seasons he made the First All-Star Team five times.

Hull played on the Million Dollar Line with Bill Hay and Murray Balfour and in 1962 became just the third NHLer to score 50 goals in a season. He won both the Lady Byng Trophy and the Hart Trophy in the 1964–65 season, won the Hart again in 1965–66, and three times captured the Art Ross Trophy. He was the First Team All-Star left-winger 10 times before leaving Chicago for the World Hockey Association in 1972.

Through the 1960s, Mikita won four Art Ross Trophies and six First Team All-Star berths. In 1966–67 he became the first player to win the Hart, Art Ross and Lady Byng trophies all in the same season, a trifecta he repeated a season later. The Lady Byng triumphs were a reversal for Mikita as he posted 154 penalty minutes in 1964–65, just 12 in 1966–67 and 14 in 1967–68.

The three All-Stars were also hockey pioneers, with Hall spending his time in Chicago refining his then-unique goaltending style, which is now considered to be a predecessor of the ubiquitous butterfly style. Mikita changed the game by introducing the curved stick blade, with Hull and his terrifying shot quickly following suit.

The trio's exploits added on-ice backing to the growing popularity of the Black Hawks' distinctive red sweaters that featured the logo of Chief Black Hawk, a major figure in Illinois history. *GQ* considers the Hawks' sweater among the top 25 in all professional sports, and in 2008 *The Hockey News* selected it as the best sweater in the NHL.

LANGWAY

2002

Rod Langway

IT WAS ONE OF THE very first team sweaters he ever wore and Rod Langway wants hockey fans to remember where it comes from.

"I wanted to honor my hometown, and it was about the only thing I had related to my hockey career from there," says Langway of the blue No. 5 Randolph High School Blue Devils sweater from Randolph, Massachusetts, which he donated to the Hockey Hall of Fame.

It was only a couple of years before he started leading the Blue Devils to conference championships that Langway had learned to skate.

"I was 13 years old and playing street hockey and other sports, but I couldn't skate," says Langway, who was born in Taiwan, but grew up in Randolph. "It was right around then that there was a hockey boom in the Boston area because of Bobby Orr. It was a home run for all of New England — from Vermont to Connecticut.

"All my buddies who played football and baseball said, 'Why don't you skate?' So I saved up money from shoveling snow and bought figure skates. I played one game on the pond and they told me I couldn't play any more because the toe picks were wrecking the ice. So I shaved the picks off. Then the next snowstorm, I saved up my shoveling money for hockey skates and bought a pair of CCM Bobby Hulls for 19 bucks."

With five older brothers, Langway was already very competitive and he simply willed himself to become a hockey player. After playing house league "with the other kids who couldn't skate," he made the town bantam team, lying about his age so he could play up a division with his older friends. Then he played three years at Randolph High School, taking the team to the Division 2 state semifinal and earning a scholarship from the University of New Hampshire for both football and hockey.

"I could drop one of them if I didn't like it," he says. "I played hockey, but I was redshirted in football, then played a season [at linebacker]."

Langway, who was selected 36th overall in 1978 by the Montreal Canadiens, opted to spend his first pro year with the Birmingham Bulls of the World Hockey Association. He then joined the Canadiens for their 1978–79 championship season. Three years later he was the cornerstone of the blockbuster trade that delivered him, Doug Jarvis, Craig Laughlin and Brian Engblom to the Washington Capitals.

The struggling Capitals had never once made the playoffs in their eight-year history and they were about to be sold and probably relocated. But the trade legitimized hockey in the American capital and rescued the franchise, and the Capitals didn't miss the postseason for the remaining 11 years of Langway's career. Langway won two James Norris Memorial Trophies along the way, relying far more upon responsible defensive play than the previous winners.

"I came in with a great bunch of players, like Scott Stevens and Mike Gartner," says Langway. "It turned out great, but I didn't win another Stanley Cup and I'd rather have two more Stanley Cups than two Norris Trophies."

CONACHER

1994

◀ Lionel "Big Train" Conacher wore this Montreal Maroons sweater during the 1936–37 season, his last in the NHL. Conacher finished his career as a Second Team All-Star on defense after recording 25 points throughout the regular season. He is shown at right playing for the New York Americans, where he spent four years of his career.

Lionel Conacher

I T'S HARD TO IMAGINE anyone having the time to accomplish what Lionel Conacher did, let alone the skill to do it.

Conacher was Canada's athlete of the first half of the 20th century — and clearly the most all-around athlete the country has ever produced — starring on teams that won the Grey Cup, the Stanley Cup, the Memorial Cup and the U.S. amateur hockey championship. He also wrestled professionally, beat Jack Dempsey in an amateur boxing match and was the runaway scoring leader in the first-ever indoor professional lacrosse league. Conacher was an early inductee into Canada's Sports Hall of Fame, Football Hall of Fame and Lacrosse Hall of Fame, and the award the Canadian Press bestows upon the Canadian male athlete of the year is named for him.

"My father's sports career was achieved in an era that will never be repeated," says Conacher's son, Brian, who played for the Toronto Maple Leafs' last Stanley Cup championship team in 1967. "The seasons were more defined. There were times he played two different sports in the same day, but generally the seasons didn't overlap much. And the players are far more specialized in all sports today."

The Conachers were Toronto's first family of sports in the 1920s and '30s, and Lionel's two younger brothers, Roy (1998) and Charlie (1961), are also in the Hockey Hall of Fame. He entered the Hall himself in 1994, a major achievement for a busy man who didn't even try skating until he was 16. Three years later, at age 19, he won the Memorial Cup

with a Toronto All-Star Team.

"The Big Train" was a large, determined defenseman who joined the NHL in 1926 with the short-lived Pittsburgh Pirates and scored their first-ever goal. He spent five seasons with the New York Americans before being sold to the Montreal Maroons, yet another now-defunct team. He spent six of his last seven seasons in two three-year stints with the Maroons. Sandwiched between those years was the 1933–34 season, which he spent with the Chicago Black Hawks. Conacher was instrumental in helping the Hawks secure their first-ever Stanley Cup championship, and after the victory he was part of a huge three-team trade that saw Montreal Canadiens superstar Howie Morenz land with Chicago and Conacher sent back to the Maroons. The Maroons, with Conacher's help, went on to win the 1934–35 Stanley Cup, the club's second.

The 1936–37 Montreal Maroons sweater pictured here was the last one Conacher wore in his hockey career. That season he finished with 25 points in 47 games for the third-highest total of his career. After the New York Rangers defeated the Maroons in the semifinal, he retired to enter politics, but not before making the NHL's Second All-Star Team and finishing as runner-up for the Hart Trophy.

"We've been very supportive of the Hockey Hall of Fame," Brian Conacher says, "although there wasn't a lot of stuff around the house because my dad wasn't a collector."

He was too busy being a player.

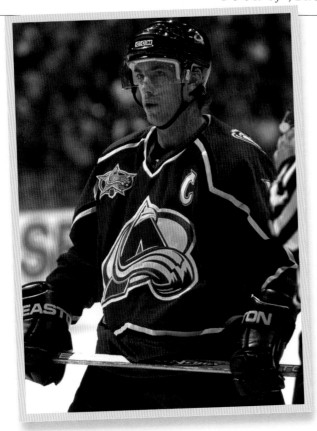

Joe Sakic (seen at left with the ▶
Colorado Avalanche) wore this Quebec
Nordiques jersey in the franchise's
final NHL season of 1994–95. Sakic
registered 62 points in the NHL lockout-
shortened season before continuing
to captain the franchise after it moved
to Colorado; with Sakic the Avalanche
won two Stanley Cups.

Joe Sakic

WHAT WAS SO EXHILARATING to their new fans in the Rockies was equally distressing to their old ones in the Laurentians.

In 1995–96 the Quebec Nordiques migrated to Denver and became the Colorado Avalanche. That season the franchise won its first Stanley Cup, which was hugged and hoisted by their lead-by-example captain, Joe Sakic, who also won the Conn Smythe Trophy.

Sakic had grown steadily into the role of exemplary leader during his seven seasons of mostly playoff-free hockey for the Quebec Nordiques — their final seven years in the NHL.

The Nordiques stood as a unique symbol within the province of Quebec: a contrast to the more corporate, more cosmopolitan and ultimately more successful Montreal Canadiens. They were the classic underdogs, trying to survive in the smallest market in the NHL and the second-smallest market in major league sport, while operating on a crippled Canadian dollar that hovered between 70 and 80 cents against the greenback.

After seven years in the World Hockey Association and 16 more in the NHL, the Nordiques may have finally lost their battle for survival, but they had used five straight years of missing the playoffs to build draft choices and create a deep roster that would win hockey's ultimate prize in Colorado only a few months after leaving Quebec.

Sakic became the Nordiques' captain in 1992–93, leading the club to their first playoff berth in six years and helping the young Nords to the greatest single-season turnaround (plus-52 points) in NHL history at the time. He continued to wear the "C" until he retired with Colorado in 2009, having scored 625 goals and 1,641 points.

Taken 15th overall with the Nordiques' second pick in the first round of the 1987 draft, Sakic requested to stay with his junior club, the Swift Current Broncos, for another year so he could hone his game for the NHL. In the process, he scored 164 points and was named Canada's major junior hockey player of the year. Patterning his game after Wayne Gretzky's creative style, Sakic became a 100-point-scorer in his sophomore NHL season and reached that mark twice more as a Nordique, averaging 1.3 points per game in his final six years in Quebec.

Winning the first Stanley Cup in Nordiques/Avalanche franchise history is the middle jewel in Sakic's drought-ending crown. In 1994 he had seven points in eight games to help Canada win its first men's world championship in 43 years; and in Salt Lake City, Utah, in 2002, he had four points in the gold-medal game and was named the tournament's Most Valuable Player as Canada won its first Olympic title in 50 years. To complete his international trophy case, Sakic also won a gold medal at the 1988 World Junior Hockey Championship and the 2004 World Cup.

The Nordiques' only championship came in 1977, when they won the WHA's Avco Cup. But even in their thinnest seasons they had created an indelible image of a team based on excitement, speed and finesse. That identity began in the WHA with players like Réal Cloutier, Marc Tardif and Réjean Houle, and continued through the team's NHL years with Peter Stastny, Peter Forsberg and Joe Sakic.

HOWE

1972

◄ Gordie Howe pulled this blue
Aeros jersey over his head for
the first time in 1973 after coming
out of a two-year retirement from
the Detroit Red Wings (whose
red jersey and winged wheel he
had worn for 25 years) to play
on a line with his two sons,
Mark and Marty.

Gordie Howe

AS THE ONLY MAN TO PLAY big-league hockey in five different decades, Gordie Howe — a.k.a. "Mr. Hockey" — built a massive memory bank of exceptional moments.

"But the day I first stepped on the ice professionally with the boys had to be the biggest thrill," Howe recalled in a 1977 interview, when he was 49 years old and still had three strong seasons left in him.

"There is no way I can possibly relate to people how it felt," he said.

The chance to play for the Houston Aeros alongside Marty and Mark, his two eldest sons, in the World Hockey Association's second season of 1973–74 pulled Howe out of a two-year retirement, which seemed premature even at the age of 43.

Two years before retiring he had scored 103 points with the NHL's Detroit Red Wings, but recurring wrist problems had forced him to move from the ice to the team's front office in 1971. His career in Detroit saw him win four Stanley Cups, six Hart Memorial Trophies and six Art Ross Trophies, and he posted a phenomenal run of 20 straight seasons in which he finished no lower than fifth in NHL scoring.

Howe was almost universally regarded as the best to have ever played the game, but he felt that he was being underused and underappreciated by the Wings after his retirement. So when the chance came to play with 19-year-old Marty and 18-year-old Mark, he jumped at it.

"How many [players], when they go on a road trip, get to take half their family with them?" Howe would later recall with great enjoyment.

Howe underwent wrist surgery in order to play with the Aeros, and the team immediately became one of the league's flagship franchises. Houston won their only two Avco Cups as WHA champions in the Howes' first two seasons with the team. The family patriarch registered 31 goals and 100 points his first year in Texas, winning the Gary L. Davidson Award as the league's Most Valuable Player. The next season the award was renamed in his honor. Mark, meanwhile, took home Rookie of the Year honors.

Howe had 368 points in four years with Houston before the family moved to the New England Whalers in 1977–78 for the final two years of the WHA. After the Whalers were the only United States–based team included in the WHA's 1979 merger with the NHL, Howe played his final NHL season, scoring 15 goals and 41 points eight years after he had originally retired from the league.

The Aeros didn't have near that kind of longevity. Originally planned for Dayton, Ohio, the franchise was bought by Texas oilman Paul Deneau and moved to Houston for the WHA's inaugural season. The Aeros stimulated hockey growth in Texas and gained a relatively large fan base with their two Avco Cup championships. But subsequent playoff disappointments and the departure of the Howes — as well as not being among the candidates for the merger with the NHL — took their toll on the team. The club left the WHA before its final season.

In 1996 the International Hockey League revived the Aeros nickname in Houston. The team plays in Texas now for the American Hockey League, and the club won the 2003 AHL championship.

LARIONOV

2008

Igor Larionov, shown at left playing for CSKA Moscow, wore this Soviet National Team jersey during early 1980s international action. Larionov was a key component of the Soviet's upset victory over Canada at the 1981 Canada Cup.

Igor Larionov

IGOR LARIONOV WAS the dominant center of international hockey for a full decade. He won two World Junior Championships and two Olympic gold medals and sublimely led the Union of Soviet Socialist Republics to its most lopsided victory over Canada in a major tournament.

Yet he never fully enjoyed hockey until he was 35 years old. At 5-foot-9 Larionov was small for a hockey player, but his on-ice comprehension, spatial awareness and sense of timing were gigantic. His intellect, curiosity and scope of interests were all similarly outsized and earned him the nickname "The Professor." Larionov was continually in conflict with repressive Soviet hockey authorities, most famously Viktor Tikhonov, the national team and Red Army coach.

After three full years with Khimik Voskresensk, his hometown team, Larionov started his mandatory military term playing for Moscow's Red Army in 1981 at the age of 20. He wanted to stay only the standard two-year term then return to play in Voskresensk, but Tikohonov had other ideas. After Larionov registered five assists against the Red Army early the previous season Tikhonov had wanted him on the Red Army club and national team, so Larionov was forced to stay.

Teamed almost immediately with wingers Vladimir Krutov and Sergei Makarov to form the KLM Line, Larionov scored 31 goals in his first Red Army season; but his line really burst into international prominence before that season began. The new trio dominated the second Canada Cup, and in the tournament final on September 13, 1981, the USSR humiliated Canada 8–1 with Larionov scoring twice, including the game-opening goal.

Studious by nature, Larionov burned inside at the restrictions of top-level Soviet hockey, which included being confined for 10 or 11 months to a Red Army hockey compound where players had little fun or even outside contact. Larionov and other veterans wanted their choice of where to play, and that was the NHL.

In the fall of 1988 Larionov wrote a 7,000-word missive to a Moscow newspaper decrying the heavy-handedness of the Soviet hockey system. He was almost immediately removed from the national team, but a players' revolt, led by Viacheslav "Slava" Fetisov, reinstated him. Larionov's defiance together with Fetisov's own public resistance led the Soviet hockey authorities to allow several Russian veterans to play in the NHL in 1989.

Larionov spent three years with the Vancouver Canucks, adjusting slowly to the NHL game, and he eventually became the line-mate and mentor of a young Pavel Bure. Highly principled, Larionov then left the NHL for a year in the Italian league so that Russian authorities wouldn't receive part of his paycheck, as they did of his NHL salary. His foot speed might have slowed, but his mind never did and he returned to the NHL to help the San Jose Sharks to a 58-point improvement in 1993–94, the largest reversal in league history.

In 1995 he was traded to the Detroit Red Wings, where he would spend the next seven seasons. Larionov said he had finally found the hockey atmosphere he had always sought, and when the Wings won the 1997 Stanley Cup — their first in 42 years — he was one of five Russian players on the team. Larionov went on to win two more Cups with the Wings and ended up playing 13 seasons in the NHL, despite playing his first game in North America just two months shy of his 30th birthday.

AROUND THE GLOBE

From Canada and the United States to Czechoslovakia and Russia, this world-class showcase of players and the jerseys they wore includes styles ranging from Seattle's early barber pole threads to the dyed and sublimated jerseys of Europe's elite leagues.

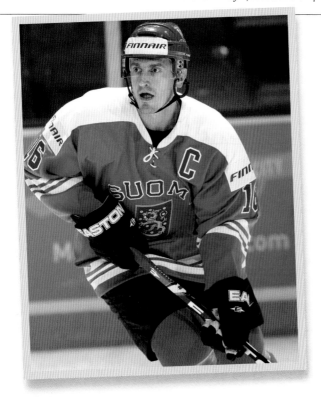

Ville Peltonen

CRAIG CAMPBELL, THE MANAGER of the Hockey Hall of Fame's D.K. (Doc) Seaman Hockey Resource Centre, says the Hockey Hall of Fame couldn't do it without Kent Angus.

Between 1995 and 2012, Angus has helped the Hall of Fame procure over 500 men's jerseys and at least 70 women's jerseys from the International Ice Hockey Federation World Championships, and he's still out there getting more.

As the operations manager for Nike Hockey, which has the IIHF apparel contract, Angus works closely with Campbell and Phil Pritchard, the Hockey Hall of Fame's vice president and curator.

"Phil and Craig give me a wish list and we do a change-out," Angus says.

In a change-out a player provides Angus, and ultimately the Hall of Fame, with his or her game-worn sweater, and receives another sweater back from Nike.

"We usually wait until the tournament to make the change-out," explains Angus. "But if it's a jersey being worn just one time, the player wears it for the warmup and the first period, and wears the second one for the rest of the game, so they're both game-worn."

The Nike resource center, usually located in an unused dressing room at the World Championship, is an active place during the tournament, especially in the early stages when teams are still solidifying their rosters after naming their original 19 players. After consulting with each competing nation on the design of its sweater and logo for that year, Nike brings 35 home and away sweaters for each country to the Worlds. Only 25 players are on the roster, but the extra stock ensures there are enough sweaters in every size to facilitate players being added to the roster and that an emergency replacement jersey is available. Numbers and names are sewn onto the sweaters as soon as the player has been officially named and sized.

"Over time we've had some [players show] reluctance to donate sweaters. Some of the players have superstitions," says Angus. "But once Phil or Craig or I talk to them and they know what it is for, it becomes a non-issue."

Ville Peltonen's sweater from the 2008 Worlds, pictured here, was historically important to Pritchard and Campbell for many reasons: it was the 100th anniversary of the IIHF; the tournament was the first men's Worlds ever held in Canada; and Peltonen, the captain of the team, has won more international medals than any other Finnish hockey player. Through 2011, Peltonen had played in a record-tying 19 tournaments for Finland, winning medals in 13 of them — no other Finnish player has more than nine. He has also been captain of the Finnish entrant at the World Championships six times.

Peltonen and the "C" seem to go together. During an elite-level career that began as an 18-year-old in 1991, the left-winger has captained the Finnish National Team, Jokerit of the Finnish Elite League, HC Lugano of the Swiss Elite League and Dynamo Minsk of the Kontinental Hockey League. And all this despite his playing three separate stints in North America over eight seasons. In total, Peltonen suited up for 382 games in the NHL — registering 184 points — before returning to Europe for good in 2009.

Peltonen holds a special place in Finnish hockey history, scoring a hat-trick in his nation's 4–1 win over Sweden for the 1995 World Championship title; the first in Finland's history.

The sweater he wore at the 2008 Worlds is just one of more than 67,000 that Nike has created for the men's World Hockey Championship since 1995.

Twenty-five-year-old Brian Kilrea wore this Springfield Indians sweater for his first American Hockey League season (1959–60), helping the Indians win their first of three consecutive Calder Cup championships. Kilrea can be seen at right with a collection of trophies; the Calder Cup is the one on the left.

Brian Kilrea

HOCKEY LORE IS DOTTED with stories of players desperate to get out of Springfield, Massachusetts, but Brian Kilrea begged to get back in.

The man who would go on to win more games than any coach in junior hockey history had finally earned a full-time role in the NHL and had already scored the expansionist Los Angeles Kings' first goal when he startled team management by asking to return to the club's farm team in Massachusetts.

"It wasn't Los Angeles or the Kings, in fact I really liked the coach, Red Kelly," Kilrea explains. "It was just too hot. I never was good with the heat, and one day I couldn't even get out of the car it was so bad."

So after 25 starts with the Kings, Kilrea returned to Springfield, where he'd become a celebrated player in a renowned hockey town.

"Saturday night was Springfield's night for hockey and they would fill the rink," Kilrea recalls of the great Springfield Indians teams of the 1960s.

The Indians were charter members of the American Hockey League when it was formed in 1936, and were purchased by the notorious Eddie Shore in 1939. Kilrea joined the Indians for the 1959–60 season, just in time to contribute significantly to the most dominant three-year stretch in league history.

Springfield won the regular-season title for three straight years and also captured the Calder Cup three straight springs. No AHL team, before or since, has done either, let alone both. It was often speculated that the Indians of 1958–59 to 1961–62 could have played in the NHL

and challenged for the playoffs. Springfield's Bill Sweeney led the AHL in scoring all three years; Kilrea scored 54 goals and added 167 assists over that span; and the defense was always stacked.

"But the heart of it all was Marcel Paille," Kilrea says. "He was the best goalie in the league."

Shore, who coached as well as owned the team, ruled the franchise with an iron fist, scheduling games on Christmas Day, running his team ragged in practice and often humiliating individual players for long stretches. And when players arrived from other teams, Kilrea recalls, they almost always had to take pay cuts "to get in line with our salary scale."

Shore's heavy-handed approach eventually resulted in serious labour conflicts, with Kilrea and lawyer Alan Eagleson representing the Springfield players. That eventually led to the formation of the NHL Players' Association and its minor league equivalent, the Professional Hockey Players' Association. Shore soon sold the team and its players to the Kings. (The original franchise eventually shifted to Worcester, Mass., in 1994 with the Springfield Falcons replacing them in the AHL.)

But Kilrea appreciated Shore's technical hockey knowledge and dedication to the game. He drew on them when he became coach of the Ontario Hockey League's Ottawa 67s in 1984. Outside of a one-year stint as an assistant coach with the NHL's New York Islanders, Kilrea remained behind the 67s bench for 35 years, coaching dozens of future NHLers, and winning 2,156 regular-season games and two Memorial Cups.

Jörgen Jönsson of Sweden's ▶
Färjestads BK wore this jersey
at the 1998 Spengler Cup.
The club finished third with a
2–2 record behind Davos and
champion Team Canada.

Jörgen Jönsson

J ÖRGEN JÖNSSON WORE HIS LOYALTIES — family and country — on his sleeve just as obviously as he wore the colors of Färjestads BK.

A left-winger who had NHL talent and proved it, Jönsson never wanted to pursue a hockey career anywhere other than in Sweden. NHL teams were made aware of his wishes, but he was still drafted; in 1994 Calgary took the then 21-year-old 227th overall.

He didn't come to North America until he was 27, and then only because the New York Islanders offered him a chance to play with his younger brother Kenny, who was then the captain of the team. The Jönssons had played together before, spending three years with hometown Rögle BK, the club they helped promote to the Swedish Elite League from the second division in 1992.

While Kenny spent 11 years in the NHL, drafted 12th overall by the Toronto Maple Leafs in 1993, his older brother rejected overtures, saying he preferred to stay in Sweden, mostly for family reasons. Even while playing with Kenny on Long Island, Jörgen hinted he would return to Färjestads at the end of the season, which he did. (Jörgen had 11 goals and 28 points in 68 games for the Islanders, and had recently been named NHL player of the week when Mike Milbury traded him to the Mighty Ducks of Anaheim at the 2000 trade deadline.)

Jörgen played 13 seasons for Färjestads — most of them as team captain — and won five Elite Series championships. But it was his international logbook that made the best reading for Swedish fans.

He played 285 international games, the most ever for the Swedish National Team, and was usually captain in games and tournaments for which Mats Sundin was not available.

Jörgen, Kenny and six of their countrymen made international hockey history in 2006 when they became the first players to win the Olympics and world championships in the same year. Jörgen completed a rare trifecta when he helped Färjestads springboard from a fourth-place regular-season finish to the Elite League championship that season. Always at his best in the bigger games, Jörgen is Färjestads' career postseason leader in points and assists, and he also scored three goals in Sweden's gold-medal run at the 2006 World Championship, the last he would play for Sweden.

His only season in North America started just a few months after he wore this sweater at the 1998 Spengler Cup in Davos, Switzerland. Färjestads finished third behind Davos and champion Team Canada. The Spengler, considered the oldest club hockey tournament in the world, began in 1923 as a vehicle for German-speaking teams that faced discrimination in the aftermath of World War I. It wasn't until 1993 that Färjestads became the first Swedish team to capture the tournament; they repeated in 1994. Jörgen, however, was still playing for Rögle with his brother that year.

Kenny returned to Rögle during the 2005 NHL lockout and stayed there until he announced his retirement in 2009, the same season Jörgen decided to call it quits after 18 years, two Olympic gold medals, two world titles and five Swedish championships.

Seattle Metropolitans sweaters worn by goaltending great Hap Holmes (top sweater, circa 1917; seen at right with the Detroit Cougars in the mid-1920s) and puckhandling winger Frank Foyston (bottom sweater, 1923–24; seen at right from this time period). Holmes, Foyston and the Mets captured the Stanley Cup in 1917, and one of five regular-season first-place finishes in 1923–24, the final season of the Pacific Coast Hockey Association.

HOLMES 1972

FOYSTON 1958

Barber Pole Dandies

LONG GONE AND RARELY CELEBRATED, the Seattle Metropolitans — not the NHL's New York Rangers — were the first U.S.-based team to win the Stanley Cup.

In March 1917, concluding just their second season in the Pacific Coast Hockey Association, the Metropolitans beat the National Hockey Association's Montreal Canadiens three games to one to win the Stanley Cup.

Seattle finished first in the four-team PCHA, which had been founded six years earlier by two of hockey's great builders, Frank and Lester Patrick. The team earned the right to host the entire 1917 Stanley Cup final, which was then a best-of-five series.

Professional hockey was evolving rapidly, and the NHA and PCHA played under radically divergent rules. The Westerners allowed forward passing in the neutral zone and played with seven men on the ice. The Easterners had already ditched the "rover" position to go with six players per side, but didn't allow forward passing. So Games 1 and 3 of the Cup final were played under PCHA rules and Games 2 and 4 were played under NHA regulations. Montreal won the opener 8–4, but the Mets swept the next three, allowing the vaunted Canadiens just one goal in each of the games. Center Bernie Morris scored 14 of Seattle's 22 goals in the series, including six in the 9–1 victory that clinched the Cup.

One of Morris' line-mates was a puckhandling winger named Frank Foyston, one of three Toronto-area players who was coaxed West when the Metropolitans were formed. Foyston had already won a Stanley Cup with the NHA's Toronto Blueshirts in 1914 and he won it again in 1925 with the Western Canada Hockey League's Victoria Cougars, the last non-NHL team to capture the Cup.

Foyston's pro career lasted 16 seasons, seven more than the Metropolitans, who finished first in 1924 but folded at the end of the season. The PCHA died with them, and the two surviving teams, Victoria and the Vancouver Maroons, shifted to the rival WCHL.

In addition to Foyston, Victoria picked up the Metropolitans' goalie, Harry "Hap" Holmes, who had originally come West to Seattle with Foyston from the Cup-winning Blueshirts. Holmes, who always wore a baseball cap to prevent fans from spitting on his bald head, also won the 1917 Cup with Seattle, and was then loaned to the Toronto Arenas (the Blueshirts' successors) for their 1918 Cup victory. He and Foyston won the Cup again with the Cougars in 1925, which made Holmes the first goaltender to win Stanley Cups with four different franchises.

Made by the Ocktoneck Knitting Company of Seattle, the woolen Metropolitans' sweaters seen here were among the most colorful of their era. The high turtleneck and rugby-like horizontal stripes reflected the sporting fashion of the early 20th century, as did the ribbon — rather than string.

GAINEY

1992

Formerly a left-winger with the Montreal Canadiens, Bob Gainey wore this jersey while playing defense as the player-coach of the Epinal Squirrels in the National 1B Division of the French Hockey League, where he recorded 26 points in 18 games. ▶

Bob Gainey

HEN BOB GAINEY WON the Frank J. Selke Trophy as the NHL's top defensive forward the first four years the award was presented, it was not because he played hockey like his dashing Montreal Canadiens teammate Guy Lafleur.

"I thought [after I retired from the NHL] if I went to a [top-tier international league] that might have been the expectation," Gainey says of his decision to end his on-ice career as player-coach of the Epinal Squirrels of the National 1B Division of the French Hockey League.

When Gainey decided to retire after the Canadiens lost the 1989 Stanley Cup final to the Calgary Flames, there wasn't much he hadn't accomplished. During his 16-year career, all spent in Montreal, he won four Stanley Cups during the dynastic 1970s while playing on the second line with Jacques Lemaire and Yvan Cournoyer; earned the Conn Smythe Trophy in the 1979 playoffs; captained Montreal to a Stanley Cup in 1986; and starred for Canada in the 1976 and 1982 Canada Cup tournaments, where his checking and skating prompted Soviet coach Viktor Tikhonov to call him the best all-around player in the world.

"I was ready to move on from my playing career, but like a lot of players I wasn't sure if I could just quit," says Gainey, "and Epinal had contacted me several times by old-fashioned mail. We went over there on a family holiday in the summer — there wasn't a real purpose to it — and decided to stay for a year."

A local savings and loan company sponsored the Squirrels. Their logo was meant to convey the idea of "squirreling money away," and advertising was everywhere on the team uniform and around the arena.

"One thing that went against my personality," laughs the notoriously private Gainey, "was that I was given a car and it had my name and the team name all over it. It was like driving a billboard. I made sure that didn't last long.

"When I got there, the team was maybe going to move or fold ... We got Epinal up and running."

With Gainey attracting attention all over France, the team survived. Today they play in France's top division under the name Les Dauphins.

Gainey likens the level of play back then to "community or senior hockey" and says he could probably have scored five points every game. As in his days in Montreal, where he became famous for hard work at both ends of the rink, Gainey focused on a team game as opposed to individual exploits like those of the Lafleurs of the NHL.

"I'd distribute the puck, try to raise the ability of the players and have some fun," Gainey says.

The coaching experience whetted Gainey's appetite and he took the Minnesota North Stars to the Stanley Cup final in 1991. He left coaching in 1995 to concentrate on managing the Dallas Stars, the new home of the relocated Minnesota franchise, and four years later was the first general manager of a sun-belt team to win the Stanley Cup.

Playing in Italy's top hockey loop, Constant Priondolo of the Alleghe Sile Caldaie wore this jersey when he broke the all-time goal-scoring record with his 372nd goal on September 30, 1989. At right he can be seen in his major junior days with Montreal of the Quebec Major Junior Hockey League.

Constant Priondolo

H E WAS DRAFTED to replace Mike Bossy, but he ended up replacing Renato De Toni.

Constant Priondolo could always put the puck in the net, which is why the Laval National of the Quebec Major Junior Hockey League made him their first choice in the 1977 Quebec midget draft after losing Bossy to the NHL. It is also why the Montreal Canadiens signed him to a three-year contract in 1981, and why he scored more goals than anyone in the history of Italian hockey.

In his eighth season in the Italian Series A with Alleghe, a town in Italy's mountainous northeast, Priondolo broke De Toni's all-time league record of 371 career goals and became the first player in Italian professional hockey to pass the 400-goal barrier. He fell just 13 goals short of 500 career goals after eight seasons with Alleghe, one with Fassa and another with the Milan Saima, and left the league in the early 1990s to concentrate on his other favorite sport, golf.

He's still celebrated for his scoring exploits in Italy, where he was known as the "Flying Italian" and the "Italian Stallion." Fans even made up a theme song for him, which they sung when a goal was essential.

In the fall of 1981 the Canadiens sent Priondolo to their farm team in Halifax, where he answered a newspaper advertisement calling for hockey players in Italy.

"They were paying about what I'd make in Halifax," he recalls. "Italy had just moved up from the World B pool to the A pool, and because of my Italian heritage, I could play in the Olympics in Sarajevo in three years. That was the main attraction: the Olympics."

He played in Sarajevo, where the Italians finished ninth. He also participated in seven world championships, the most memorable by far in Finland in 1982.

Against a prohibitively favored Canadian team that had Wayne Gretzky in its lineup, Priondolo scored to give Italy a 3–2 lead before the Canadians rallied for a tie late in the game. Canada lost a medal because of that unanticipated draw, and Italy, which also beat the United States, became the first team promoted to the A pool since it was expanded to eight teams to not be relegated the next year.

At 5-foot-6 and 160 pounds, Priondolo was small for the NHL, but his speed and blistering shot allowed him to score 39 goals in his first season in the Italian Series A when De Toni, in his 16th and final year, was also on the Alleghe roster.

When the owner of the Milan team died and his heirs were slow to decide whether the club would play in 1992–93, Priondolo accepted an offer to play in the U.S. with the Sunshine Hockey League's Daytona Beach Sun Devils. He had a winter home nearby and had just earned his Canadian Professional Golfers' Association card. He ran the hockey operations for Milan for three more winters after that, but concentrated more on golf. Today he is the head pro at Vallée du Richelieu in Montreal.

Geoffrey Hallowes, captain of the Cambridge University Ice Hockey Club, wore this sweater in 1939, and likely wore it for the Cambridge-Oxford Varsity Match, the oldest continuous hockey rivalry in the world.

Geoffrey Hallowes

ALTHOUGH THE DARK CLOUDS of war were gathering when Geoffrey Hallowes wore this iconic English sweater, he could not have imagined how dramatically his life was about to change.

Soon to become a war hero, Hallowes was the captain of the 1939 Cambridge University Ice Hockey Club, which has since been recognized as one of the oldest hockey teams in the world and is credited for helping plant an interest in hockey among athletes in continental Europe in the late 19th and early 20th centuries.

Rosters and photographs of the team date back to February 1895, and although no hard historical evidence exists, it is believed that a Varsity Match between Cambridge and bitter rival the University of Oxford took place in St. Moritz, Switzerland, 10 years earlier, with Oxford prevailing 6–0.

The first official Varsity Match between the two venerable schools was played using bandy sticks and a lacrosse ball at the Prince's Skating Club in London in March 1900. Oxford won that year; Cambridge the next. And in 1903, Cambridge became one of five founding teams — all based around London — of Europe's first formal hockey league.

By 1909 the Varsity Match was part of a European tour, a tradition that lasted until 1931, when both Cambridge and Oxford became founding members of the English Hockey League. Besides Oxford and Cambridge, the league iced a combined team from both the Prince's and the Queen's sports clubs known as the Manchester Lions, as well as a team of transplanted Canadians who played their games in the banquet hall of the Grosvenor House Hotel in front of well-heeled diners.

When the English League folded in 1936 most of the teams joined the new English National League, but Cambridge — by then no longer able to compete with the emerging professionals — opted to compete in the lower-level London and provincial leagues. Cambridge and Oxford still continued the annual Varsity Match.

The late 1930s were a heady time for hockey in England as Canadian-stocked Great Britain upset Canada for the 1936 Olympic championship, and an influx of Canadian players had made the English National League arguably the second-best league in the world. National League matches featured live music and figure-skating exhibitions, while the leading theatre stars of the era were among the many patrons at rink-side.

The first televised hockey game in the world was a National League game between the Harrington Racers and the Streatham Redskins in late October of 1938. At this time Hallowes was not only the captain of the Cambridge squad, but the club president as well; the Varsity Match that season was also aired on television in 1939.

With the outbreak of World War II, Hallowes was commissioned as an officer and served in the Far East, surviving the disastrous Battle of Singapore. Later he was parachuted into France to work with resistance fighters and was awarded the Croix de Guerre Avec Palmes for his bravery. After the war, he married one of Britain's most famous war heroes, Odette Churchill, who had been mercilessly tortured by the Gestapo and survived a concentration camp.

Hallowes died in 2006, the year of the 116th Oxford-Cambridge game. It is the oldest continuous hockey rivalry in the world, with Oxford winning roughly two-thirds of the games, partially because of its Canadian Rhodes Scholars, but also because Cambridge, despite its unique and enduring place in the game's history, has never had its own rink.

GRANATO

2010

◀ **Cammi Granato, who had an illustrious international career and is shown at right skating for Team USA, wore this Vancouver Griffins jersey for the club's inaugural National Women's Hockey League home stand on October 25, 26 and 27, 2002. Despite Granato's four points the Griffins lost all three matches.**

Cammi Granato

REAMS DO COME TRUE, but sometimes they aren't exactly as imagined.

After realizing she would probably never get to play in the NHL, Catherine "Cammi" Granato took a break from playing hockey during her last two years of high school. She "was crushed" that her brothers were able to chase their dreams and that she could not.

But a little more than 20 years later — after personifying the stupendous growth of female hockey in the United States — Granato was "in awe" as she and Angela James were the first two women inducted into the Hockey Hall of Fame.

Growing up near Chicago with five older siblings — four brothers (including future NHLer Tony) and a sister — Granato had always taken playing hockey with the boys for granted. She skated on male teams until she was 15, when bodychecking became prevalent and the boys' increasing size and strength started to take its toll. In high school, when her vision of playing for her hometown NHL Chicago Blackhawks apparently ended, she turned to other sports for two years.

But a new hockey dream presented itself when Granato was offered a scholarship to hockey powerhouse Providence College in 1989, just as women's hockey took its fledgling steps into international play.

She was Freshman Player of the Year and, as co-captain, eventually led the Providence Friars to the Eastern College Athletic Conference championships in 1992 and 1993. In her four-year college career Granato scored 135 goals and added 110 assists in just 93 games.

And when the U.S. formed a women's national team, Granato was one of its first members and became its longest serving player. She won

a silver medal at the first Women's World Championship in 1990 and played in every world championship through 2005.

Blessed with extraordinary leadership skills, Granato quickly became the most recognizable female hockey player in the U.S., if not the world, and was a deeply trusted spokesperson and role model for the women's game.

Although indelibly associated with American women's hockey, Granato played for Concordia University in Montreal, Quebec, for three years after graduating from Providence College, and led the team to three consecutive Quebec titles, with 326 points in 123 games. When she finished her master's degree in 1997 the timing dovetailed nicely with the formation of the yearlong American National Team program, which led into the 1998 Winter Olympics, the first Olympic Games to include women's hockey.

Granato captained the 1998 U.S. Olympic team, scored the team's first goal of the Games and led the Americans to an upset gold-medal win over world champion Canada.

After winning a silver medal at the 2002 Olympics, Granato captained the Vancouver Griffins in 2002–03, the team's only season in the National Women's Hockey League. The Griffins went 27–4 to finish first in the West, although they were eliminated in the first round of the playoffs. Living in Vancouver, British Columbia, with her husband, former NHLer Ray Ferraro, she continued to play for the U.S. National Team until she was released, in a controversial decision, before the 2006 Olympics. Not long after that she was enshrined as a member of both the International Hockey Hall of Fame and United States Hockey Hall of Fame, with the ultimate recognition of the Hockey Hall of Fame in 2010, making yet another unlikely dream come true.

BENEDICT

1965

Game-changing goalie and Stanley
Cup–champion Clint Benedict wore
this Windsor Bulldogs sweater
is his last professional hockey
season (1930–31) while leading the
Bulldogs to the International Hockey
League championship. He can be
seen at left as a member of the
Montreal Maroons.

Clint Benedict

I N THE EARLY NHL, whenever goaltending history was made Clint Benedict was somewhere in the immediate vicinity. Benedict is best remembered for designing one of the first crude goalie masks in 1930 and wearing it for only one game before discarding it — but he was a precedent-setter long before that.

Hockey had banned goaltenders from dropping to the ice to stop shots, however Benedict's creative avoidance of the rule led the NHL to abandon it when the new league was formed in 1917, with Benedict's Ottawa Senators as charter members. Other goalies had already followed his lead, smothering loose pucks by pretending to be knocked onto their knees, thus circumventing the two-minute penalty. Angry Toronto fans gave Benedict his "Praying Bennie" nickname for reportedly kneeling on the ice to "thank the heavens."

And although Benedict wasn't the first goaltender to be credited with an NHL shutout, he was the second, blanking the Montreal Canadiens and their goalie Georges Vézina 8–0 on February 25, 1918, just a week after Vézina had recorded the new league's first whitewash. Two years later, Benedict's five shutouts were the only ones recorded in the NHL that season.

While Vézina and his Canadiens successor, George Hainsworth, carry the larger reputations from the early NHL years, it was Benedict who dominated the statistics, just as his Senators dominated the standings. His 2.66 goals against average in 1919–20 was 2.13 goals per game better than the league average, a margin that has never been equaled. He led the NHL in wins in six of the league's first seven seasons, and the Senators — whom Benedict joined as a 20-year-old in

1911 when they were in the National Hockey Association — captured three Stanley Cups in four seasons between 1920 and 1923.

Despite his success, Benedict was sold to the new Maroons franchise in Montreal; the Senators justified the sale of their star goaltender by pinning their unexpected exit from the 1924 playoffs on his drinking problem. Benedict responded with six excellent seasons in Montreal, leading the Maroons to the Stanley Cup in just their second year — still a record for an NHL expansion team. He allowed only three goals in the four-game final against the Victoria Cougars, becoming the first goalie to win Stanley Cups for two different NHL teams. Quick and combative, he posted 13 shutouts in 1926–27 and 11 more two years later.

While Benedict wore modified cricket-style shin guards even after Emil "Pop" Kenesky had invented the first version of modern goal pads, he was ahead of his time on other technology. Soon after a Howie Morenz shot knocked him cold in early 1930, Benedict unveiled the NHL's first goalie mask: a leather face covering with an enlarged, fortified nose covering. He wore it in only one game, though, blaming his 2–1 loss on the mask. Later that season, another Morenz shot hit him in the throat and by the following season, he was waived to the Bulldogs, the Maroons' International Hockey League team in Windsor, Ontario.

The Bulldogs, one of many noted Windsor senior and professional teams to carry the nickname, were an IHL powerhouse, packed with former and future NHLers, and in his final year of playing hockey Praying Bennie won another league championship.

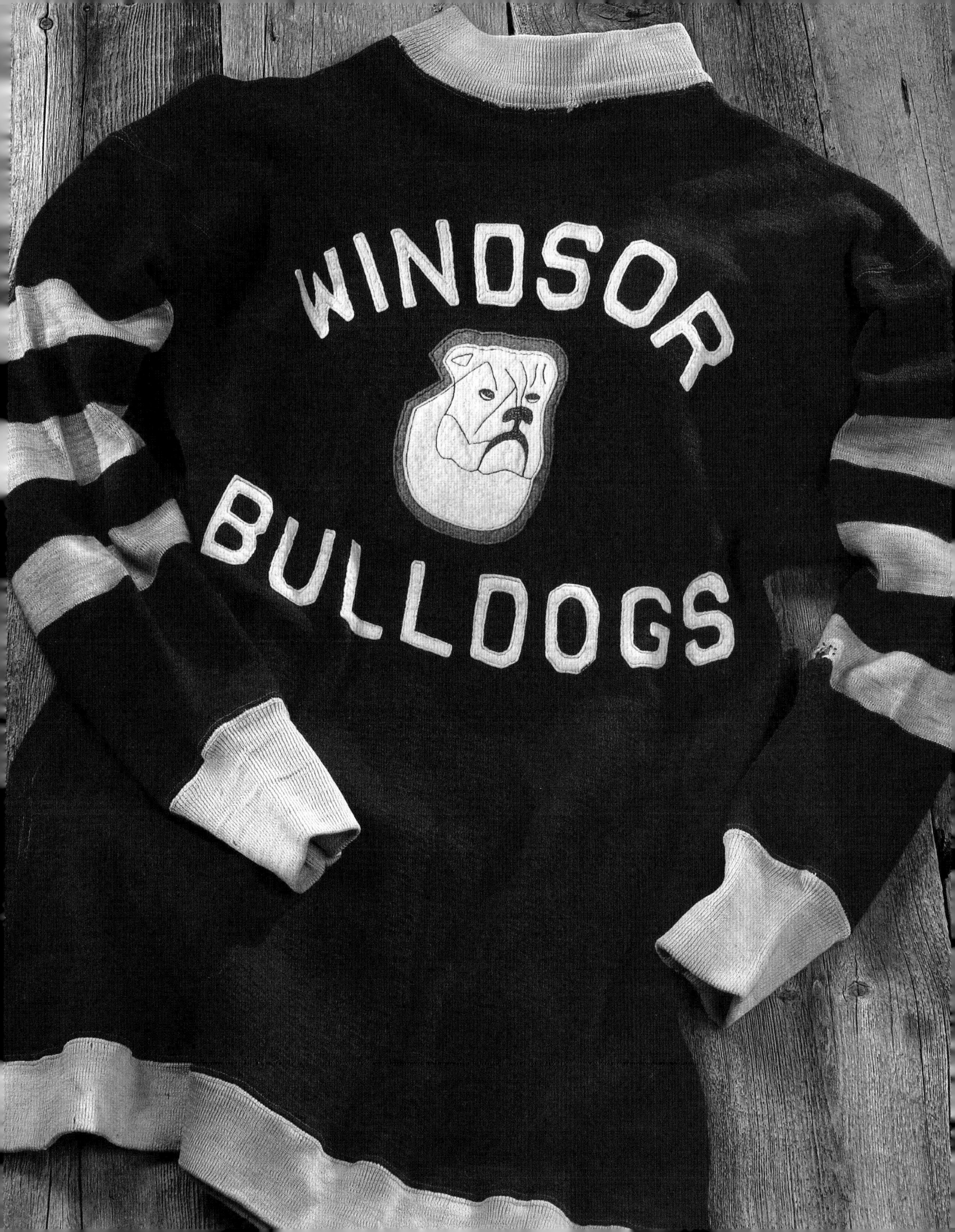
WINDSOR
BULLDOGS

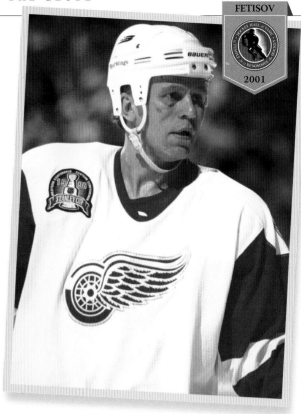

FETISOV

2001

◄ Viacheslav Fetisov wore this Union of
Soviet Socialist Republics jersey while
representing his nation internationally –
most likely at an Izvestia Cup tournament.
During this time, Fetisov was stripped of the
team captaincy by coach Viktor Tikhonov.
Fetisov openly quarreled with USSR hockey
authorities and eventually led the charge for
Russians to play in the NHL, himself playing
in New Jersey and then in Detroit, where he
won two Stanley Cups.

Viacheslav Fetisov

HEN HE WAS STILL a junior player, Viacheslav "Slava" Fetisov dared to take far more offensive chances from the blue line than the Soviet hockey system dictated, and the system eventually changed because of him.

And that is the perfect metaphor for how Fetisov conducted his broader life.

Fetisov, captain of both the powerful Moscow Red Army team and the Union of Soviet Socialist Republics' national team, risked his hockey career and future lifestyle in the late 1980s by openly challenging the communist government and eventually blazing the trail for himself, and many Russians after him, to play in the NHL.

As the greatest defenseman in Russian hockey history, Fetisov is one of six former national-team teammates elected to the International Ice Hockey Federation's Centennial All-Star Team. Elected alongside him were longtime blue-line partner Alexei Kasatonov and the legendary KLM Line of Vladimir Krutov, Igor Larionov and Sergei Makarov. The quintet formed the USSR's "Big Five," or "Green Unit," and together they were the centerpiece of most of the Soviet Union's seven World and two Olympic championships won in Fetisov's career.

In 1978, five months after Fetisov had led the Soviet Union to its third straight World Junior Championship (winning the award for the tournament's best defenseman for the second year in a row), the Montreal Canadiens played a long shot and selected him with the 201st pick of the 1978 NHL draft. They didn't expect him to ever play in North America — and neither did the New Jersey Devils, who chose him 150th overall when he was re-entered into the draft in 1983.

But Fetisov was as fierce, determined and skilled off the ice as he was on it.

"It was not easy, but I kept battling until I won," he recalls.

Fetisov supported Larionov in his 1988 battle with Soviet hockey authorities and left the Red Army after its 1989 North American tour against NHL teams, one of which was the Devils. He had already spoken openly against the heavy-handed regime of Soviet hockey and had been threatened by authorities with criminal charges and banishment to one of the USSR's hockey outposts. But when national team leaders announced that Fetisov would not be eligible for the 1989 World Championship, his teammates rallied behind him and said they would not play without their captain. In effect, they threatened a players' strike.

Because of his untouchable national stature — and with the reforms of the Glasnost policy coloring the larger political picture — the government gave in and Fetisov became one of the first Soviet citizens to receive a visa to work in the West. He and seven other veterans were permitted to come to the NHL, with the proviso that they would return to play for the national team.

Although he was 31 years old when he first suited up for New Jersey, Fetisov contributed eight goals and 42 points to the Devils in the 1989–90 season. Traded to the Detroit Red Wings late in the 1994–95 season, he helped them win back-to-back Stanley Cups in 1996–97 and 1997–98 before retiring as one of four players ever to win the Stanley Cup, a World Championship, an Olympic championship, the Canada/World Cup and a World Junior Championship.

Fetisov's entire, difficult journey came full circle when he took the Stanley Cup home in 1997, the first time the NHL's top trophy had ever been to Russia.

Darren Boyko played 11 seasons with Helsinki IFK, for whom he wore this jersey during the 1993–94 season. While in Europe, Boyko played for Team Canada at the Izvestia Cup and played against Team Canada at the Spengler Cup. ▶

Darren Boyko

IT CERTAINLY WASN'T HIS DREAM as he grew up playing shinny on the large rink his father had built in the family's backyard.

But by the time he hung up his skates in 1997, Darren Boyko had played more games (476) in the Finnish SM-liiga than any other foreign player and retired with the most foreign-player points (406 points: 171 goals and 235 assists).

"The quality of life was great, it was terrific for our family," Boyko recalls. "And the hockey was fantastic. It improved my game and gave me my opportunity, at the age of 24, to crack an NHL roster."

After his first three years with Helsinki IFK, the only Finnish team he played for in his 11 years in the league, Boyko signed a contract with his hometown Winnipeg Jets in 1988. He was a healthy scratch for a few games, then after he played his one and only NHL match that October, the Jets wanted to demote him to the minors. However, Boyko's contract allowed him to return to Finland for the balance of the schedule — and that's what he did. He later fulfilled his Jets' contract by reporting to Winnipeg's American Hockey League farm team, the Moncton Hawks, late in the season.

Boyko had originally gone to Finland, and before that to the University of Toronto, where he won a national title under coach Mike Keenan, hoping to find "some different sets of eyes" to scout him. He had gone through two NHL drafts unselected, despite scoring 84 goals and 202 points in his first two years with the major junior Winnipeg Warriors.

"Certainly size was an issue," says the 5-foot-9 Boyko. "And it could

be that scouts made assessments that my skating was average and my shooting was average."

Whatever the reasons, HIFK was glad Boyko had been overlooked. He joined the team figuring he and his wife, Trish, would be in Helsinki "at the most, seven months," but he delivered an excellent rookie season and earned a second one-year contract. The only time in his 11 seasons with HIFK that he signed for longer than one season was from 1993 to 1995, when he was also completing a master of business administration at Helsinki's International School of Economics.

HIFK shares a home arena with Jokerit, and games between the two tenants still set the city abuzz.

"It's like the Mets and Yankees in New York," explains Boyko. "The fans are not on the fence. You can't like both teams: you choose. The media ate it up and the players felt the intensity and pressure."

When the team changed direction under a new manager in 1996, Boyko played one more season with the Berlin Capitals in Germany and then retired. German hockey, he explains, was different than the Finnish hockey of the time because imports were expected to carry most of the play rather than blend into a skilled unit.

"Finnish hockey was great," Boyko says. "When I first got there it wasn't as professional, with guys going to school or having jobs, but the last five or six years it was very professional."

Boyko is now the business development manager for the Hockey Hall of Fame, working closely with the International Ice Hockey Federation.

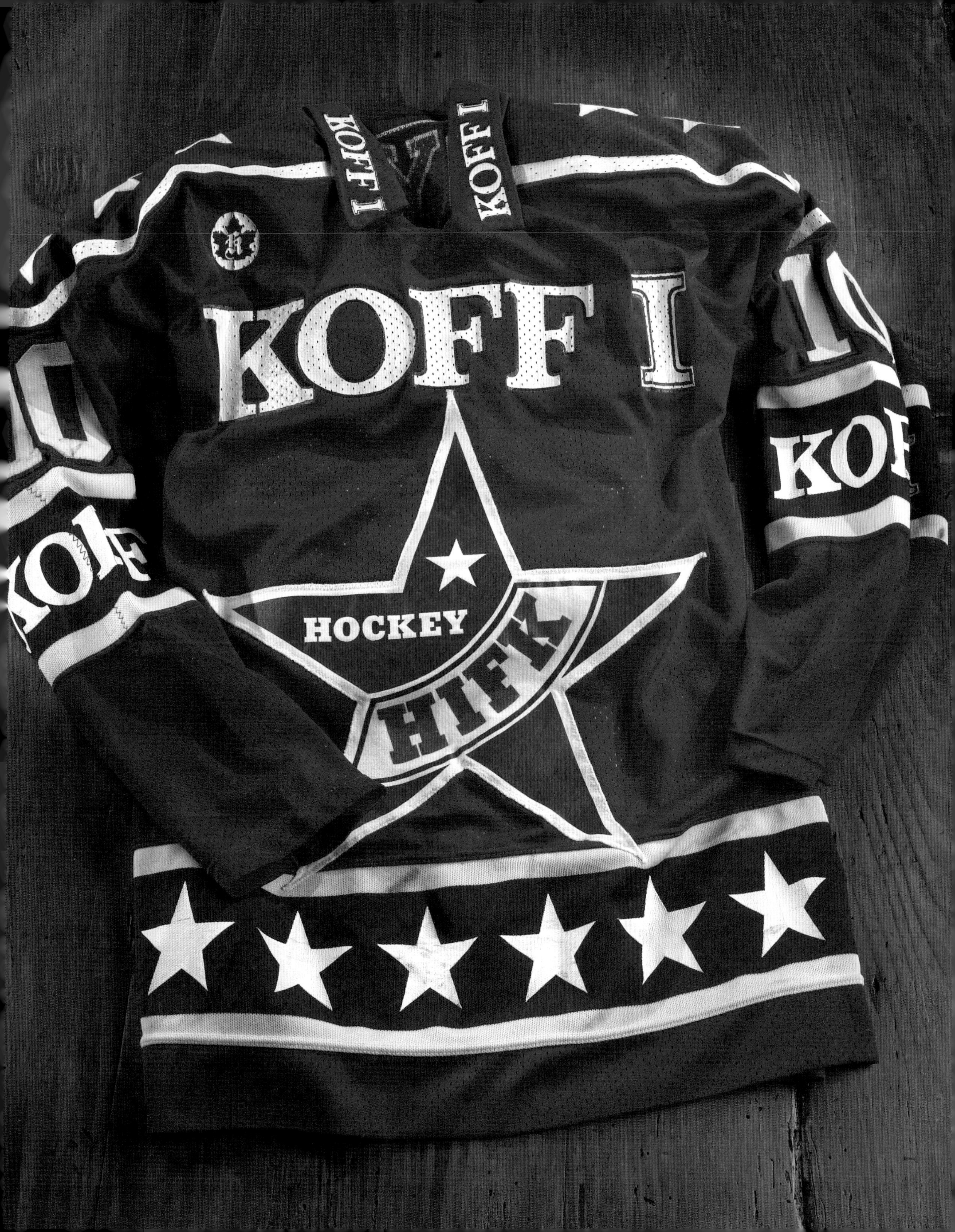
KOFF I
KOFF I
KOFF I
10
10
KOFF
KOFF
HOCKEY
HIFK

◀ **Larry Murphy, newly converted from center to defense for the Don Mills Flyers, wore this jersey throughout the 1977 Wrigley National Midget Tournament held in Moncton, New Brunswick. The Flyers defeated Quebec's Lac St. Louis Lions 7–6 in the gold-medal game to claim the championship.**

Larry Murphy

L ARRY MURPHY FOUND OUT early on that if a door gets closed in your face you should have a look around, because a window's got to be open somewhere.

The man who retired from the NHL with the most games played by a defenseman — and the second most points scored — might never have moved back to the blue line if the famous midget team he was trying out for hadn't been so deep down the middle.

"I was a minor midget trying out for center, but the coach had convinced a lot of midget-aged guys to stay back from Junior B and it was pretty crowded there," says Murphy of the Don Mills Flyers, the 1977 Wrigley National Midget Hockey Tournament champions.

"I wasn't going to make it, but the coach, Don Booth, said, 'We've got a couple of positions on defense, so why don't you try there?'"

Murphy jumped at the chance and helped the Flyers win the Wrigley tournament, which had begun only two years earlier and has continued to this day under various sponsorships.

That was his second year with the Don Mills organization after getting cut from the Toronto Marlboros' minor system. What had originally seemed like a setback resulted in the trip of a lifetime for Murphy.

"[The Flyers] got to play in Czechoslovakia and in Russia when it was still the Soviet Union. What an experience," he says.

After capturing the Wrigley, the Flyers dropped out of their Toronto league to barnstorm against Ontario Junior B, C and D teams in an attempt to ramp up the competition level before heading overseas. It was a prescient strategy as Don Mills went 3-1-0 in the Soviet Union — including a 5–3 victory over the Red Army juniors — and 3-1-1 in

Czechoslovakia.

The teenage players had been advised by international travelers to take along extra pairs of blue jeans, as well as gum and peanut butter, which were in short supply behind the Iron Curtain.

"You traded them for rubles on the black market, and I bought fur hats and little toy Russian bears as souvenirs for everyone back home," Murphy recalls.

After his Wrigley season, Murphy played a year of Junior B, then was drafted by the Ontario Hockey League's Peterborough Petes. Peterborough won the Memorial Cup under coach Gary Green in Murphy's first year. In his second season as a Pete, the club made it to overtime of the final game of the Memorial Cup under now-legendary coach Mike Keenan.

He had already become one of the NHL's top all-time scoring defensemen, winning two Stanley Cups with the Pittsburgh Penguins, before his career brought him full circle and he landed back in his hometown in 1995 for two seasons with the Toronto Maple Leafs.

Toronto would finish 14 games under .500 in 1996–97, and the fans took out their ire on Murphy. Late that season Murphy waived his no-trade clause, not because of the Leafs' fans but because of the Detroit Red Wings' promise.

"I thought we would turn it around in Toronto," says Murphy, who was traded to the Wings. "But Detroit was too good an opportunity to turn down."

He climbed through that open window to help the Wings to their first Stanley Cup in 42 years. When Detroit won again in 1998, Murphy became the only player to win four Cups in the 1990s.

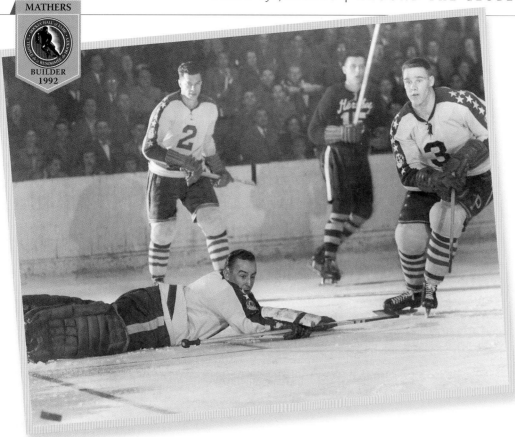

Frank Mathers wore typical digits for a defenseman of the 1950s, but there was nothing typical about his play. Between the American Hockey League's Pittsburgh Hornets (No. 2) and Hershey Bears (No. 3), Mathers won four Calder Cups and was named to the First All-Star Team five consecutive times. At left, Mathers and Pittsburgh Hornets teammate Tim Horton watch a puck deflect wide in a game against the Hershey Bears.

Frank Mathers

NOT ALL LEGENDARY HOCKEY careers are forged in the National Hockey League.

Frank Mathers was already famous in American Hockey League circles before he arrived in one of America's best hockey cities in 1956. Hershey, Pennsylvania, is among the most enduring and stable markets the AHL has ever had; and its Hershey Bears are considered the AHL's cornerstone franchise, in large part because of what Mathers accomplished in "Chocolatetown" over his 35 years as a player, coach and executive.

Mathers was an all-around athlete who played professional football before he reached the professional ranks in hockey. He lined up at fullback for both the Winnipeg Blue Bombers and Ottawa Rough Riders of the Canadian Football League, and played in a wartime Grey Cup game for the Winnipeg Royal Canadian Air Force Bombers.

Signed by the Toronto Maple Leafs as a defenseman, Mathers played only 23 NHL games, scoring just one goal. But in 1948, when the Leafs sent him to their AHL affiliate in Pittsburgh, Mathers really began to make his hockey name. Playing in the antiquated Duquesne Gardens and wearing red sweaters that resembled football jerseys with numbers on the front, the Pittsburgh Hornets were nevertheless an AHL power in the first half of the 1950s.

They won their first Calder Cup in 1952 over the Providence Reds in double overtime in Game 6. The Hornets reached the final again the next year, and in 1955 Mathers won his second Calder Cup in four seasons.

In 1956 the team's rink was torn down and the franchise suspended operations until a new rink was built five years later. Then 32, Mathers considered retiring, but was lured to Hershey by the Bears' persuasive manager John Sollenberger, who talked him into becoming the team's player-coach.

Mathers responded by making the All-Star Team in each of his first five seasons, which included back-to-back Calder Cup championships in 1958 and '59. When he retired as a player in 1962, he had become the all-time AHL defensemen's points and assists leader, and the Bears retired his No. 3 jersey. Including his six years as player-coach, Mathers held the Bears' reins for 17 years and coached them to another Calder Cup in 1969. Moving into the general manager's office for another 18 years, he took the club to another three Calder Cup championships, making it 15 appearances in the Cup finals, including six championships, in his 35 years in Hershey.

Mathers has become as synonymous with Hershey as their distinctive maroon sweaters, which — like those of most dynastic franchises — are instantly recognizable.

"When I first came to the league [in 1987], Frank was to the American Hockey League what Gordie Howe was to the National Hockey League," recalls AHL president Dave Andrews. "He was the most famous player we had in the league, and he was equally as important as a builder in Hershey. Frank is truly a legend. The American Hockey League has been all about the Hershey franchise, and the Hershey franchise is all about Frank Mathers."

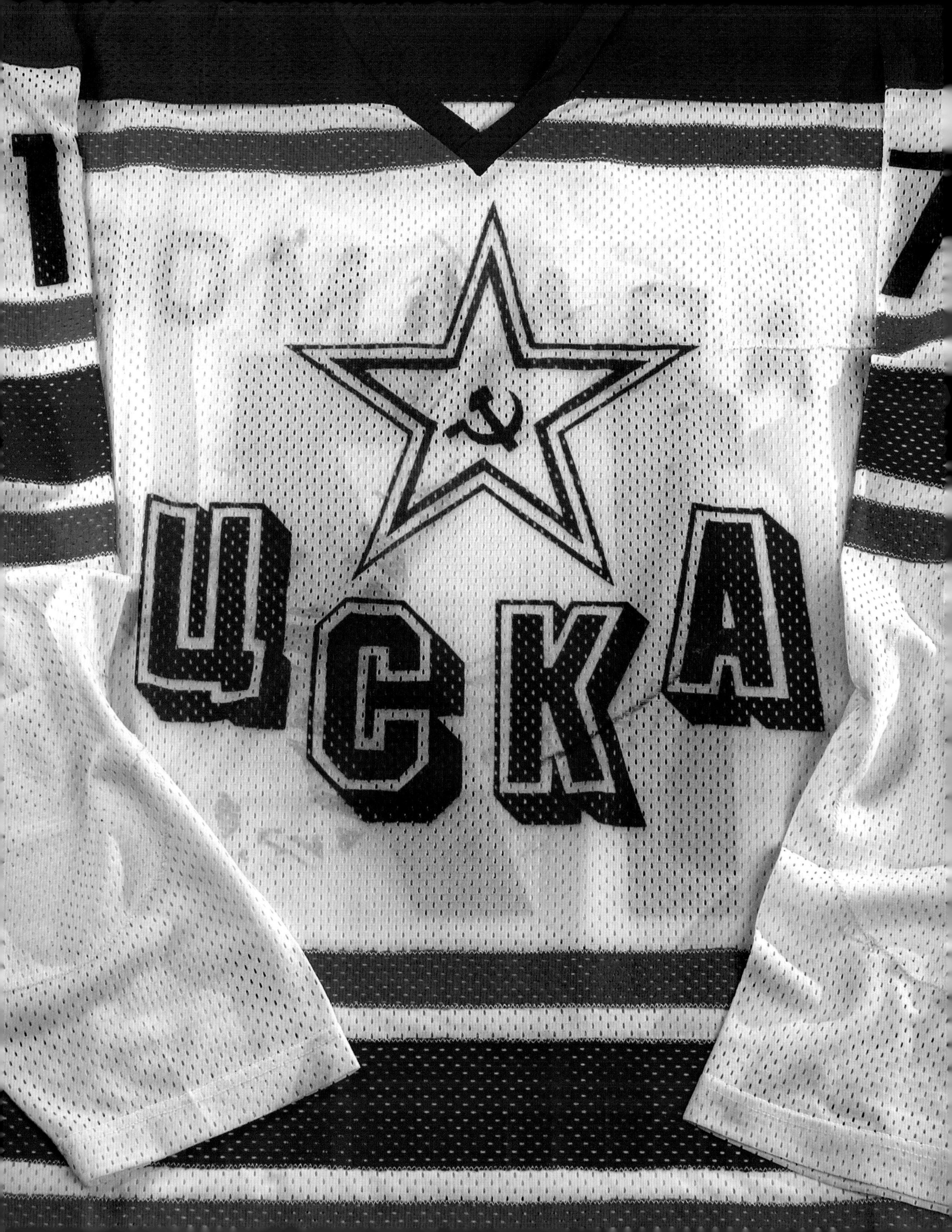
ЦСКА

Lokomotiv Yaroslavl star Ivan Tkachenko, shown at right in red, wore this sweater for the 2002–03 Russian Hockey League season and playoffs, helping his team capture its second straight Russian championship. Tkachenko was captain of the team in 2011 when the entire Yaroslavl team perished in a plane crash.

Ivan Tkachenko

HAD IT NOT BEEN FOR the most horrible of circumstances, his kindness may have gone unrecognized forever.

On September 7, 2011, Ivan Tkachenko, captain of the formidable Kontinental Hockey League power Lokomotiv Yaroslavl, transferred 500,000 Russian rubles to the family of a young cancer patient, part of a series of donations he was making anonymously to help save the lives of critically ill children.

Only a few minutes later, Tkachenko and 43 others, including the entire Lokomotiv playing roster and coaches, were dead when their Yakovlev Yak-42 airplane crashed just after takeoff.

Lokomotiv, the Russian national champion in 1997, 2002 and 2003, and who had reached the third round of the KHL playoffs the two years before the crash, was traveling to Minsk that day for the team's regular-season opener.

Among the victims were several players who had also played in the NHL, including the 1999–2000 Lady Byng Memorial Trophy winner Pavol Demitra, who had led Lokomotiv in scoring during the 2010–11 season. Brad McCrimmon and Igor Korolev, ex-NHLers about to embark on their Russian coaching careers, were also among the passengers.

The hockey world mourned widely and deeply. With NHL camps about to open, the bulk of players were taking part in informal workouts with teammates when news of the fatal crash reached them. Most had trouble digesting the reality of so much death within the hockey fraternity, where paths cross time and time again over a career.

"Guys just going to work and playing the game they love, and something like that happens? We fly all the time, and to see a guy that I actually knew … it's hard to deal with," says the Toronto Maple Leafs' Colby Armstrong, who had played for McCrimmon in both Atlanta and Saskatoon.

Among the dozens of tributes that took place across several countries, was an NHL regular-season game in mid-October between the Pittsburgh Penguins and the Washington Capitals, where players from both teams wore Lokomotiv commemorative patches. The ceremonial faceoff featured Mario Lemieux dropping the puck for the top two Russian players in the NHL, Alexander Ovechkin and Evgeni Malkin.

Rather than return to the KHL with a roster of borrowed players for the 2011–12 season, Lokomotiv decided to participate in the Vysshaya Hokkeinaya Liga, the top feeder league for the KHL for a season. The 9,000 tickets for Lokomotiv's first VHL game (a 5–1 victory against Neftyanik Almetyevsk on December 12, 2011) sold out in four hours.

Owned by the state railroad operator, Lokomotiv has been in existence since 1959 and played in the second division of the old Soviet hockey system for 24 years before being promoted to the top tier in 1983. A new arena was built for the team in 2001, a year after the team's name was changed to Lokomotiv. The Yaroslavl team had gone by several previous nicknames.

Tkachenko, a left-winger who was selected in the fourth round of the 2002 NHL draft by the Columbus Blue Jackets but who never played in the NHL, had been with the team since 2001 and played an all-around game, contributing 10 to 15 goals each season.

It was only after the crash that friends and family members spoke up about Tkachenko's long-term generosity. He had never wanted even his teammates to know about the donations he made to sick children, which had surpassed 10 million rubles with his last gift, the timing of which defies description.

Bill Hutton, born in Calgary, Alberta, started his career with the junior Calgary Canadians and worked his way to the professional ranks with stops with Ottawa and Boston of the NHL before his 21 games with the Philadelphia Quakers in 1930–31. He rounded out his career in Vancouver, British Columbia, with several solid seasons in the minor-pro Pacific Coast Hockey League.

Bill Hutton

THEY ARE THE TEAM that time forgot.

Besieged by disappointing attendance and financial woes as the Great Depression tightened its grip, the Philadelphia Quakers spent only one season in the NHL, memorable only for their unprecedented ineptitude. The team then quietly disappeared into the mists of history, and so did NHL hockey in Philadelphia, Pennsylvania, until the expansion Philadelphia Flyers joined the league in 1967, reviving and making respectable the orange and black colors that were associated only with mediocrity when the Quakers wore them.

The Quakers were cursed by franchise DNA: Although lightweight boxing legend Benny Leonard was allegedly the team's owner, he was really the front man for bootlegger "Big" Bill Dwyer, who also owned the New York Americans. Dwyer and Leonard moved the Pittsburgh Pirates, who were part of the NHL from 1925–26 to 1929–30, to Philadelphia for the 1930–31 season and changed the team name to the Quakers.

The duo hoped to use the new name to play upon several favorable local images to help build a fan base for the team: city founder William Penn was a Quaker; the popular Philadelphia Phillies of baseball's National League had been officially known as the Quakers from 1883 to 1886; and four years before the NHL team moved to town the Philadelphia Quakers had won the 1926 championship of the original American Football League. The football Quakers went down with the AFL the next year, a partial omen of what was to happen to the hockey team.

The Quakers set several futility records. Two years earlier, in Pittsburgh, the Pirates had missed the playoffs by 21 points, and in their final season in Pittsburgh they had gone only 5-36-3 to miss the playoffs by 31 points. But the Quakers were even worse: They didn't score a goal until their third game, lost 15 games in a row from mid-November until mid-January and had a .136 winning percentage, missing the playoffs by a whopping 35 points. The league suspended the team for a year, then killed the franchise for good in 1936 without ever having revived it. The losing streak and miniscule winning percentage stood as NHL records until 1974–75, when the expansion Washington Capitals broke both marks, stimulating a brief flurry of historical interest in the Quakers' fruit-fly existence.

"Nobody knew about them," says Rod Hutton, who donated the sweater of his grandfather, Bill Hutton, to the Hockey Hall of Fame in 1994. "I said to my dad, 'This sweater has to be one of a kind,' so we contacted the Hall, and they said they'd never seen a Quakers' sweater. We donated it to the Hall, as well as some pictures and programs from that era.

"It was just sitting in a cedar hope chest the whole time I was growing up," Rod says.

Bill Hutton was a defenseman and right-winger who was 20 when he was traded to the Quakers before the 1930 season after spending two years with the Boston Bruins and Ottawa Senators. Although he had only one goal and one assist in his 21 games with Philadelphia, he was an aggressive checker and one of the few bright spots — along with future Hall of Famer Syd Howe — on the worst team of the NHL's first half-century. Hutton spent another dozen years earning a good living in the top minor leagues around the continent.

Hutton's Quaker sweater was valued at $10,000 in 1994, and Ebbets Field Flannels has manufactured a replica jersey.

"We bought them for the whole family," says Rod Hutton. "And they gave us a really good deal. After all, they wouldn't have had the template if it wasn't for us."

ALL-STARS

An All-Star Game is a unique opportunity for a league to honor its best players; it is also, in most cases, an occasion to create a unique garment. This collection of selects ranges from the most prominent professional leagues to the smallest minor-pro and junior circuits.

Mike Bossy, pictured at right in his New York Islanders uniform, wore this sweater while accepting a new car that he earned as All-Star Game MVP for his two goals (including the game winner) that led the Wales Conference team 4–2 over the Campbell Conference All-Stars in the 1982 All-Star Game.

Mike Bossy

ONLY A SNIPER OF Mike Bossy's unparalleled accuracy would consider 38 goals a failure.

But Bossy's goal-scoring standards were so high — by some measurements the best of all time — that when chronic back troubles limited him to 63 games and 38 goals in the 1986–87 season, he knew he should retire.

But no one would have considered his retirement a possibility six years earlier in 1981–82. That year, Bossy — who surpassed the 50-goal mark in every season but his shortened 1986–87 campaign — broke the 60-goal barrier for the third time and set the scoring record for right-wingers with 146 points. Halfway through that record-breaking campaign Bossy took the ice at the All-Star Game wearing this sweater and scored two goals in the Wales Conference's 4–2 win and was named game MVP.

It was only four years earlier, in 1977–78, that Bossy had made his NHL debut. Islanders' head coach Al Arbour assembled what would go on to become the New York Islanders' most prolific line ever, with center Bryan Trottier and massive left-winger Clark Gillies. The Bossy-Trottier-Gillies trio skated their way right into NHL history as Bossy became the first NHL rookie ever to score more than 50 goals in a season, finishing with 53.

Nicknamed "The Long Island Lighting Company," the line was constructed from classic building blocks: a brilliant two-way center in Trottier, who could pass creatively to both sides; an aggressive muscular left-winger in Gillies, who could dig pucks out of the corner and also score; and a right-winger in Bossy, who many say was the most

naturally gifted shooter in the history of the game. It was Trottier's perfect pass which Bossy whipped past Quebec Nordiques goalie Ron Grahame in 1981 to become the first player since Maurice "Rocket" Richard in 1945 to score 50 goals in 50 games.

"A lot of us put up a lot of points because of Mike Bossy," says Denis Potvin, who along with goalie Billy Smith and The Long Island Lighting Company was one of the five pillars of the Islanders dynasty. "You knew if you could get him the puck, it was in the net."

Especially on the power play. Thirty-two percent of Bossy's 573 goals came with the Islanders enjoying a manpower advantage. That success, in turn, made other teams less aggressive for fear of taking penalties, creating another advantage for the Islanders. Many Islander fans argued that New York's opponents weren't penalized nearly enough for the manner in which they tried to neutralize Bossy's ability to score. His career-ending back problems likely originated with the physical abuse he absorbed on the ice.

Bossy became the first major star of the modern era to criticize the violence in NHL hockey, warning that it was subjecting the game to public ridicule in the United States. Although he had often stood up for himself after continuous on-ice attacks as a prolific junior scorer in the Quebec Major Junior Hockey League, many scouts saw him as soft and weren't sure he could last in the NHL. He was still available for the Islanders 15 selections into the 1977 draft.

Bossy played the game the way he wanted others to play it, averaging only 21 penalty minutes a season and winning three Lady Byng Memorial Trophies in his career — all while being one of the most feared shooters in the history of the NHL.

GIACOMIN

1987

Robbie Irons' No. 30 jersey, worn in the 1973 IHL All-Star Game, was a hand-me-down from the NHL. The top-flight pro league used this style All–Star jersey for many years, ending in 1972. Ed Giacomin wore this sweater at the 1971 NHL mid-season classic when representing the New York Rangers. Both netminders can be seen at left; Irons in his brief stint with the St. Louis Blues.

Hand-Me-Downs

LONG BEFORE IT BECAME popular — and necessary — the NHL was into recycling.

"For our All-Star Game, they used to give us their sweaters from their All-Star Game the year before," says Robbie Irons, the longtime netminder for the Fort Wayne Komets who wore sweater No. 30 in the 1973 International Hockey League All-Star Game.

Irons' IHL All-Star sweater is of the same vintage and style as Ed Giacomin's NHL Eastern Conference All-Star sweater (both of which can be seen here), a design that the NHL had used for several years, ending in 1972.

It's uncertain whose 1972 NHL sweater Irons inherited for the 1973 IHL game. Gilles Villemure, Giacomin's New York Rangers goaltending partner, was named to the 1972 NHL roster and wore No. 30, but looking at Irons' No. 30, the "0" is quite faded when compared with the "3." This could be because Irons continued to wear his jersey after the game and washed it many times: "I wore it outside in the backyard like a pullover," he explains. It could also be that the "3" had been sewn onto the sweater's front, back and arms to make a new sweater for Irons out of another All-Star jersey. If this is the case, the jersey was likely originally worn by either Gilbert Perrault (No. 10) or Dallas Smith (No. 20).

Giacomin, who became one of the most popular players in New York Rangers history, wasn't on the 1972 NHL All-Star Game Eastern Conference roster, as Villemure and the Montreal Canadiens' Ken Dryden were awarded the two goaltending berths. But Giacomin and Villemure had been the two Eastern Conference goalies for the 1970 and 1971

games, and in the spring of 1972 they shared the netminding chores — with Giacomin getting more starts — as the Rangers made the Stanley Cup final for the first time in 21 years. Unfortunately for Giacomin and Villemure, the Rangers lost in six games to the Boston Bruins.

Giacomin and Irons had crossed paths early in their professional careers. When Irons made the jump to the NHL in the 1967–68 season, Giacomin had a lock on the Rangers job and New York sent Irons, who had suffered a broken arm, to the Fort Wayne Komets. The St. Louis Blues traded for Irons in 1968, where he was third on the depth chart behind Glenn Hall and Jacques Plante. In fact, Irons played exactly three minutes and one second for the Blues in the 1968–69 season. Hall was ejected and Plante, his replacement, wasn't ready, so Irons had to go into the net.

Irons returned to Fort Wayne for good in 1970 and, while Giacomin endeared himself to New York fans, Irons was doing the same thing in Indiana. He made the All-Star Team in six of his 11 IHL seasons, and like Giacomin, the team retired his number.

Among North America's pro teams, only the NHL's Original Six and the American Hockey League's Hershey Bears have played continuously in the same city longer than the Fort Wayne Komets. It is such a welcoming hockey environment that more than 40 team alumni still live in the area. Bob Chase has called home and away games on WOWO 1190 AM since the team's inception in 1952.

"WOWO was 50,000 watts when I played," Irons recalls, "and my family in Toronto could hear every one of my games clear as a bell." Since retiring from the game in 1981, Irons has been working home games as Chase's broadcast partner.

Nels Stewart, shown at right with the Montreal Maroons, wore this torn and moth-eaten Ace Bailey Benefit Game sweater on February 14, 1934. Stewart registered a goal and an assist in the All-Star's 7–3 loss to the Toronto Maple Leafs. The game raised $20,000 for Bailey and his family.

Nels Stewart

IT TOOK 14 MORE YEARS before it evolved into an official fun-fest, but the NHL All-Star Game really began with a near tragedy.

Twelve days before Christmas in 1933, in the second period of a game in Boston Garden, Eddie Shore was checked hard by the Toronto Maple Leafs' tough defenseman Red Horner. Woozy and confused, the combatant Boston Bruins superstar thought he was getting back at Horner, but instead slammed Ace Bailey to the ice. The popular Leaf was knocked unconscious with a skull so severely fractured that a priest administered him the last rites. Boston police threatened to charge Shore with manslaughter if Bailey didn't survive, but neurosurgeons worked all night and saved his life, though he could never play hockey again.

Prompted by a suggestion from a Montreal sports writer, the NHL staged a benefit game for Bailey and his family at Maple Leaf Gardens on Valentine's Day, 1934. The Leafs played a collection of NHL All-Stars, and Bailey's No. 6 became the first number retired by an NHL team. Bailey presented each player with his sweater, and one of hockey's most poignant moments came when he extended a sweater, and his hand, to Shore.

Bailey also gave NHL president Frank Calder a trophy he hoped would become part of an annual league All-Star Game to help injured players, but that idea was too far ahead of its time.

The Leafs defeated the selects 7–3 with the first All-Star goal going to Nels Stewart. There was a certain irony in Stewart's participation:

nicknamed "Old Poison," he was one of the most truculent and feared players in the NHL.

Stewart was a laborious skater, but he had a terrifying shot and was deadly around the net. At 6-foot-1 and nearly 200 pounds, he used physical intimidation as an effective weapon. When Stewart won the NHL scoring title and was named the league's Most Valuable Player as a rookie with the Montreal Maroons in 1925–26, his 119 penalty minutes were more than double what any other top-10 scorer incurred that year. But his 34 goals represented 37 percent of the Maroons' offense and stood as a rookie record for 55 years. That year's playoffs Stewart scored six of Montreal's 10 goals, as the second-year franchise won the Stanley Cup over the Victoria Cougars.

Beginning in 1929–30, Stewart was the pivot between his boyhood friend Hooley Smith and Babe Siebert on the legendary S Line, where he scored 39 goals to help win his second Hart Trophy as league MVP. Stewart finished his career with the New York Americans, and in 1936–37, his first season with the club, he won the scoring title 11 years after he captured his first one. When he retired in 1940 his 324 goals stood as an NHL record until Maurice "Rocket" Richard blew by it thirteen years later.

Stewart didn't play in either the 1937 Howie Morenz Memorial Game or the 1939 Babe Siebert Memorial Game. Along with the Ace Bailey Benefit Game, those games formed the foundation for the NHL's first official All-Star Game, held at Maple Leaf Gardens in October 1947.

Jody Gage, representing
the Rochester Americans,
captained the U.S. squad at
the 1995 AHL All-Star Game,
the first such contest for the
league since 1959. The game
has since had three formats:
U.S. teams versus Canadian
teams, Canadian players versus
PlanetUSA (everyone else) and
most recently, East versus West.

Jody Gage

I F DAVE ANDREWS HAD come along earlier, Joseph "Jody" Gage might have played in 17 American Hockey League All-Star Games.

He played in only one, but it's probably fitting that the resurrection of the AHL's mid-season classic coincided with the last full year of the AHL legend's playing career. Until 1995, the only thing Gage hadn't accomplished in the AHL was a starting berth in the All-Star Game.

When Andrews took over as president of the AHL in the 1994–95 season, he envisioned a new image for the league. He wanted to make the league younger and he wanted it to be the undisputed feeder league to the NHL, with every team having its top farm team in the loop. That year, the AHL had 16 teams; there were 26 in the NHL. A bidding war for veteran players was taxing both the AHL and its rival, the International Hockey League. By the early 2000s, the IHL was gone and the AHL had 30 teams, each with a parent NHL club.

Andrews wanted to showcase the AHL product, so on January 17, 1995, in Providence, Rhode Island, All-Star Teams representing the league's 10 United States–based franchises met the selects from the six Canadian-based teams. Gage, in his 11th season with the Rochester Americans, was a co-captain for the American side.

"I'm from Toronto, and my grandmother was watching the game on TV and basically calling me a traitor," Gage laughs.

The AHL staged six All-Star Games between 1954 and 1959 before abandoning the concept for 36 years.

In its absence, Gage was building a spectacular AHL résumé. He played only 68 NHL games in his career, but in his six seasons with the Adirondack Red Wings (the Detroit Red Wings affiliate) and the following 11 with the Buffalo Sabres farm team in Rochester, New York, Gage became the third-leading goal and points scorer in AHL history. He set the league record with seven seasons of 40 goals or more, holds the playoff goal-scoring record and, in 1987–88, scored 60 goals — one shy of the league record.

It was for the 1985–86 campaign that George "Punch" Imlach had lured Gage away from the Red Wing chain with a bonus for every goal over 40. "I made out pretty well on that one," says Gage, who eventually became general manager of the Rochester Americans and is still a club executive.

"I don't have any regrets about not playing more in the NHL because I had a great career, and how can you complain about that?" says Gage. "I had a great quality of life and wouldn't change it for anything. I'm a rarity: a guy who spent all that time playing, with only two organizations. And I'm still with one of them."

Gage resisted going to the IHL, despite being offered substantial contracts, because he felt a loyalty to "the city, franchise and fans in Rochester," he says. "I am very proud of the American Hockey League. Dave had the right idea to make it a full development league and he stayed with it."

Andrews feels equally as strong about Gage's contribution to the league.

"When you look at the 'new' AHL, Jody Gage's would be the most significant career," says Andrews. "He was to his era what Frank Mathers was to the 1950s."

◄ Cleveland Barons star forward
Norm Locking wore this sweater
in the AHL's first-ever All-Star
Game, staged to support the war
relief effort. Locking recorded
an assist in the game as his
Western Division squad lost 5–4
to the East.

Norm Locking

IT WAS SUPPOSED TO BE the first annual, but instead it just became the first.

On February 3, 1942, the American Hockey League staged an All-Star Game with select players from its East and West Divisions meeting head-to-head at the Cleveland Arena.

The game was a minor swell amid the waves of patriotism sweeping the United States three months after Pearl Harbor, and the idea was to raise funds for both the American and Canadian Red Cross relief efforts for overseas servicemen. It preceded by three days a similar effort from mostly retired NHL players at the Boston Garden.

The AHL game was more official than the one in Boston, with a committee of fans, players and media selecting the players from the league's 10 teams. Former New York Rangers superstar Frederick "Bun" Cook, the coach of the Providence Reds, was behind the bench of the Eastern All-Stars, who included the celebrated Eddie Shore in their lineup. Cook's equally famous brother Bill handled the Western selects.

Bill Cook's Cleveland Barons had won the Calder Cup as league champions the previous spring — in the first season that the league had shortened its name from the International American Hockey League — and the Barons were justifiably well represented with five players in the All-Star Game.

Among the popular Baron quintet was their top line of center Les Cunningham, right-winger Joffre Desilets and left-winger Norm Locking. Desilets, who had previously spent five years in the NHL, scored two of

the West's goals with Locking drawing an assist in the East's 5–4 victory.

Locking, who was from Owen Sound, Ontario, had played 52 games, with just two goals, for the NHL's Chicago Black Hawks in the mid-1930s. He arrived in Cleveland from the IAHL Syracuse Stars in time for the 1940–41 schedule and contributed 25 goals and 44 points to the Barons' championship season. He remained in Cleveland for another three seasons and scored 26 goals in 1942–43, his penultimate year. Due to injuries, he played only 19 games the next season, registering 18 points, and he retired after the season.

Given the enormous popularity of the team in Cleveland — games there regularly drew 10,000 fans — many critics thought the AHL's All-Star Game should have featured the league champion Barons against All-Stars from the other nine teams, a format the NHL adopted with its first official All-Star Game in 1947 and that the AHL used when it resumed All-Star Games in the 1954–55 season.

As it was, there were more than 6,000 empty seats in the Cleveland Arena. But the 3,580 who did attend contributed $5,000 to the coffers of both Red Cross societies.

Despite the small crowd, the league had planned to continue the benefit All-Star Games on a yearly basis and probably would have changed the format. But the following year the war effort and its economics began severely affecting U.S.-based teams, with some losing their arenas to military needs. By the middle of the 1942–43 season, the AHL was down to seven active franchises, putting an end to All-Star Game talk until well after World War II was over.

Chris Caulfield of the West Palm Beach Blaze wore this jersey as he and his Sunshine Hockey League All-Stars skated in a three-game series against the Russian Elite League's Yaroslavl Torpedo in January 1995. The SuHL All-Stars lost all three games. Caulfield can be seen at left celebrating between teammates Scott Garrow (left) and Don Stone (right) after winning the 1993–94 SuHL title.

Chris Caulfield

BILL FRIDAY, THE SUNSHINE Hockey League's commissioner for most of its brief life, describes the loop as "very, very primitive. I'd class it as a Junior B league with older players."

The former NHL referee tried to improve the conditions, refereeing and playing caliber of the Sunshine Hockey League, but the small Florida-based circuit was undercapitalized and lasted only three seasons from 1992–93 to 1994–95. In 1995–96 the league changed its name to the Southern Hockey League and expanded to include other southern states, but it was too little too late and the league folded at the end of the season.

In the wake of Wayne Gretzky's trade to the Los Angeles Kings and the NHL's rapid expansion into sun-belt markets, a number of minor-league teams and even entire leagues sprung up like mushrooms in nontraditional areas, and Florida was no exception.

The Sunshine Hockey League began with teams in West Palm Beach, St. Petersburg, Daytona Beach and Lakeland, and halfway through its inaugural season somehow saw fit to add another team in St. Petersburg. Constant Priondolo, a former Daytona Beach Sun Devil, recalls that the player draft "was kind of just pulling the names out of a hat." In the league's final year they even experimented with a team out of Fresno, California, that played a limited schedule.

"It was a terribly run league," says Friday. "They didn't have the money. They didn't even have a commissioner, so I said I'd help out. But after a while they stopped paying me and I stopped being commissioner." Friday recalls that the home team always provided the visitors with pizzas for the bus rides home. "It was that kind of league," he says.

The one success story was the West Palm Beach Blaze, which former NHLer Bill Nyrop ran until his premature death from cancer at the age of 43 on January 1, 1996. The Blaze won the regular-season title and playoff championship each of the league's three seasons, and when the league's one and only All-Star Team was selected to play a top Russian team, the Blaze were well represented.

Among the Blaze's stars was winger Chris Caulfield from Belmont, Massachusetts, whose only professional stop after graduating from Salem College was the three years he played in West Palm Beach.

"He may not be flashy, but he gets the job done," Nyrop said at the time.

Standing eighth in league scoring, Caulfield was on the SuHL select team that played Yaroslavl Torpedo on three consecutive nights in Lakeland, West Palm Beach and Jacksonville in early January 1995.

At the time, Torpedo stood second in the Russian Elite League when it left for North America, and had four of the top six Russian scorers from the previous season. They were also the only Elite League team to defeat a team of Russian NHLers who toured the Soviet Union during the NHL lockout in the late fall of 1994. Torpedo toured the United States with three players — Andrei Tarasenko, Dmitri Krasotkin and Oleg Komissarov — who were also members of the national team.

The touring Russians won all three games handily — a surprise to no one. But the chance for the SuHL players to take on a team of such caliber was definitely a unique experience. Torpedo continued on to face American university teams as well as professional teams from the American Hockey League. Later that same year the SuHL's Daytona Beach Sun Devils traveled to France for a weekend tournament against international competition a little closer to the SuHL skill level.

◀ Jim Johnson donned this
sweater as his Manitoba Junior
Hockey League All-Star squad
won the Charles Gardiner
Memorial Trophy for their 6–2
victory over the Saskatchewan
Junior Hockey League All-Stars
in 1962. Johnson went on to
play 11 professional years split
between the NHL and the World
Hockey Association.

Jim Johnson

VERY FEW CITIES IN CANADA in the early 1960s could match the vibrancy of the junior hockey scene in Winnipeg.

"We had four teams in the city and one in Brandon, all of them sponsored by NHL teams," recalls right-winger Jim Johnson, who played for the Winnipeg Rangers before going on to an 11-season professional career that included 186 points in the NHL. "Three of the Winnipeg teams, some years all four, would play out of the Winnipeg Arena, so they'd often have doubleheaders there."

The oldest junior league in the country, the Manitoba Junior Hockey League was established after World War I as the "Winnipeg and District League," with nine teams suiting up for its inaugural 1918–19 season. By the 1960s, however, the league was down to five teams with another Manitoba franchise, the Flin Flon Bombers, playing in the Saskatchewan Junior Hockey League.

An All-Star Game within a five-team league would have provided thin fare, so the MJHL and SJHL staged their first of a series of annual All-Star Games between the leagues on January 21, 1962, at the Winnipeg Arena. The highly anticipated game between rival hockey-crazy provinces attracted 7,044 fans, and NHL president Clarence Campbell traveled all the way from Montreal to represent the NHL.

"I think they were also trying to start more communication between the Saskatchewan and Manitoba leagues," recalls Johnson, who scored a goal in Manitoba's 6–2 victory in the inaugural cross-border game. "In those years we never really saw the teams from Saskatchewan because the way the Memorial Cup playdowns were set up, we'd play the Lakehead winners from Ontario while Saskatchewan and Alberta were also playing off."

Johnson finished eighth in scoring during the 1961–62 MJHL season. League goal-scoring champion and future NHLer Marc Dufour of the Brandon Wheat Kings scored twice in the All-Star Game, as did his Wheat Kings' teammate Gerry Kelly. Paul Allan of the St. Boniface Canadiens added a single, while on the Saskatchewan side Ron Willy of the Estevan Bruins and future NHLer George Swarbrick of the Moose Jaw Canucks tallied goals.

Others who played in the game and would eventually suit up in the NHL were Peter Stemkowski of the Maple Leafs–owned Winnipeg Monarchs, Brandon's Ted Taylor and Johnson's Winnipeg Rangers teammate Bob Woytowich.

With all that firepower, the Brandon Wheat Kings were about to embark on a three-year MJHL championship run, replacing Johnson's Rangers, who had made it to the 1961 Memorial Cup semifinal before losing to the Edmonton Oil Kings.

"When we played Brandon in the Manitoba championship, there were more than 10,000 in the Winnipeg Arena for all three games there," Johnson recalls. "Junior hockey was really big in Winnipeg in that era. But when the pro team (the Jets) came it kind of fell off."

By then, the MJHL had become a Junior A league; Canada's junior leagues had become segmented into Major and Junior A divisions in 1970, the Major division representing top-level junior hockey. After Johnson returned from a professional career that included 302 NHL games and another 157 in the World Hockey Association, he rejoined the MJHL, spending three years behind the bench of the St. Boniface Saints, the franchise that had originally been his Winnipeg Rangers. Johnson also went on to spend five years as assistant coach of the University of Manitoba women's program.

CHAMPIONS

Whether an All-Star or a fourth-line role player — once a player is crowned a champion he always remains a champion. This collection, worn by all manner of players and designed in all manner of styles, encompasses professional, amateur and international champions.

What a difference 50 years makes. In his wool sweater (bottom), Al Purvis, along with the rest of the Edmonton Mercurys, won gold for Canada at the 1952 Olympics. Fifty years later, Jarome Iginla and the hand-picked squad of NHLers chosen to represent Canada donned the most current athletic gear as they worked through some early tournament adversity to bring home the gold for the first time since the Mercurys did it in 1952.

50 Years in the Making

EVEN THOUGH JAROME IGINLA'S team won the game, it sure didn't seem like they would be able to end the 50-year drought that stretched all the way back to Al Purvis' time.

Expectations and anxiety were both running high for Iginla's Team Canada when they faced the lowly regarded German team in their second game of the 2002 Winter Olympic tournament at Salt Lake City, Utah.

At the previous Olympic Games (Nagano, Japan, in 1998), Canada had finished out of the medal standings in what was the first Olympic tournament to involve the full participation of the NHL. And in their opener at Salt Lake, Canada was humbled 5–2 by a Swedish team that appeared to be the best team in the tournament. On February 17, 2002, when Iginla wore this sweater, Canada saw their 3–0 second-period lead over the German team narrow to one goal in the third period. The Canadians managed to hang on and edge Germany for an unflattering 4–2 win, but a tie in the next game against the Czech Republic did little to instill confidence in a team trying to bring home Canada's first men's hockey gold medal since 1952.

With Canada 1-1-1 and a minus-2 in goal differential, it appeared that Salt Lake would be another Canadian disappointment. But team general manager Wayne Gretzky made an emotional speech at a news conference, Pat Quinn provided a steady coaching hand, Martin Brodeur became the undisputed number one goalie and a Canadian ice maker secretly buried the now-legendary Lucky Loonie at center ice — all of which helped Canada get by both Finland and the surprising Belarus team and into the gold-medal game against the host team, the United States.

There Iginla and line-mates Simon Gagné and Joe Sakic stepped to the forefront. Iginla and Sakic each scored twice in a thrilling 5–2 victory, and Iginla assisted on Sakic's game winner. (Eight years later Iginla would also assist on Sidney Crosby's gold-medal winner at the 2010 Vancouver Olympics.)

It's fitting that Iginla played such a huge role in Salt Lake. Although he played for the Calgary Flames, he was born on Canada Day in Edmonton, Alberta — the city that had sent the intermediate Edmonton Mercurys to win Canada's previous gold medal, 50 years to the day (February 24) of the 2002 triumph.

The Mercurys won the 1950 World Championship and were chosen for the 1952 Olympics by the Canadian Amateur Hockey Association from seven nationwide bidding teams.

There were no playoffs in that Olympic era, but when the tournament came to its final day, the undefeated Canadian side, which had outscored its seven opponents 68–11, led the second-place Americans by two points in the standings. The U.S. needed a victory to win their first Olympic gold, but even with a furious late charge they had to settle for a 3–3 tie and the silver medal.

Al Purvis, an assistant captain for the Mercurys, was a strong-checking defenseman in his third year with the club. Like a number of his teammates, he worked for Waterloo Mercury, the Edmonton car dealership that sponsored the team. After the Games he returned to the dealership and eventually became its owner.

With the Mercurys' victory, Canada had won five of the first six Olympic gold medals. No one suspected they'd have to wait five decades to bring home another Olympic gold.

WORLDS
CHAMPIONS
1922-23

CHAMPIONS
OF THE
WORLD
1920-21

Frank Nighbor won the Stanley Cup four times in his 15 years as an Ottawa Senator. The jerseys here were worn following Cup triumphs in 1920–21 and 1922–23. The Senators were unable to defend their title either season they wore the championship garb.

Frank Nighbor

FRANK NIGHBOR SPENT HIS post-hockey career in the insurance business, but he had won so many trophies he could have just as easily gone into hardware.

Nighbor possessed a skill set of seemingly opposing traits. He was fast and energetic, but he was also among the last of the "60-minute players" who never really left the ice. He was a prolific goal-scorer, but he was also known for his defensive prowess as professional hockey's first expert at the poke check. For a gifted scorer he took a lot of penalties, but he was also considered the most gentlemanly player of his era.

In fact, in 1925 when Evelyn Byng — the Viscountess Byng of Vimy and wife of Canada's governor-general — decided to donate a trophy to the NHL, to be awarded to the player exhibiting the most sportsmanship, gentlemanly conduct and skill, she chose Nighbor as the first winner. Lady Byng and her husband, Lord Byng, loved hockey and often watched Nighbor's Ottawa Senators. Nighbor was awarded the Lady Byng Trophy in its second year of existence as well.

In 1923, two years prior to his first Lady Byng win, Nighbor was named the first winner of the Hart Trophy, which was initiated by the fledgling NHL to honor its Most Valuable Player. And when Howie Morenz won the Hart Trophy in 1928, just two years before the end of Nighbor's career, he is reputed to have said, "I won the trophy, but Nighbor is the greatest player in hockey."

Although Nighbor played for and starred in other high-profile teams in four different top-level leagues, it's fitting that he is best remembered as an Ottawa Senator, because he grew up not far from Canada's capital in Pembroke, Ontario.

He left Pembroke for Port Arthur, Ont., and scored six goals in his first senior game, then as a 19-year-old joined the Toronto Blueshirts of the National Hockey Association and scored 25 times in 17 games, including six times in one night against the powerful Montreal Wanderers. Lured west to the Pacific Coast Hockey Association, Nighbor played for the Vancouver Millionaires on a line with Frederick "Cyclone" Taylor and averaged better than a goal a game. When Vancouver won the 1915 Stanley Cup in a three-game series with the Senators, Nighbor scored five times.

The following year he returned home to play for the Senators, who were on the verge of becoming the game's dominant team. Nighbor and the Quebec Bulldogs' Joe Malone each scored 41 goals in just 19 NHA games in the 1916–17 season.

Two years after helping found the NHL in 1917, the Senators started a run of three Stanley Cups in four seasons, a mark that wouldn't be matched until the late 1940s by the Toronto Maple Leafs. Nighbor's moth-eaten sweater from 1921–22 shown here displays the "Champions of the World" patch that the Senators wore for winning their second Stanley Cup in 1920–21. His sweater from 1923–24, which commemorates the 1922–23 championship season, is also pictured. As if it were bad karma, each season the Senators wore these "championship" sweaters, they were unable to defend their title.

Nighbor won another Cup with Ottawa in 1927 and retired in 1930 after spending the last half of that season with the Toronto Maple Leafs. After coaching for a few seasons, he returned to Pembroke to his insurance partnership, carrying a lot of hardware.

John Coward won an Olympic ▶
gold medal wearing this jersey
when he and his Great Britain
teammates finished the 1936
Olympic tournament as the top
team. Ensuring their victory was
a decisive 2–1 win over Canada
in the semifinal round. Coward is
shown at left (kneeling, third from
left) with the Richmond Hawks of
the English National League.

John Coward

THE 40-YEAR SPARRING MATCH between British ice-hockey promoter John "Bunny" Ahearne and Canadian hockey authorities arguably originated at the 1936 Winter Olympics in Garmisch-Partenkirchen, Germany.

Canada had entered the fifth Olympic hockey tournament as prohibitive favorites, capturing gold at the previous four Games without losing a match and amassing a 202–8 goal differential.

But Ahearne, the Irish-born secretary of the British Ice Hockey Federation, had other ideas for Garmisch-Partenkirchen. He assembled a team of players who were playing in the English National League but who were either born in Canada or had grown up and learned the game there.

The Canadian Amateur Hockey Association had suspended 16 players for not securing releases to play in England, and two of them, scorer Alex Archer of the Wembley Lions and game-changing goaltender Jimmy Foster of the Richmond Hawks, were on Britain's 1936 Olympic roster. Citing the Olympic spirit, Canada relented and dropped the suspensions — thus enabling Archer and Foster to participate at the Games — sportsmanship that would come back to haunt Canada and its representative team, the Port Arthur Bearcats.

Foster, before migrating to the Richmond Hawks in England, had led the Moncton Hawks to the 1933 and 1934 Allan Cup titles. In Richmond, one of his teammates was left-winger John "Red" Coward, whose Olympic sweater is pictured here.

Foster was born in Glasgow, Scotland, and Coward in Ambleside, England, but both had immigrated to Canada with their families at an early age. Coward grew up in Rainy River, Ontario, which is only 270 miles from Port Arthur, Ont., so he was familiar with the Bearcats. He moved back to his birth land in time to play for Richmond in the 1935–36 season.

But even without lifting the suspensions, Canada's 1936 Olympic pursuit was marred from the outset. The players on the 1935 Allan Cup champion team, the Halifax Wolverines — who, following tradition, should have been the club that represented Canada at the Games — had mostly dispersed to other teams, and those who remained wanted expense money to compete. So the runner-up Port Arthur Bearcats, bolstered by four extra players, were sent to Garmisch-Partenkirchen instead.

In Great Britain's now-legendary second-round 2–1 victory over Canada, the first British goal was scored just 40 seconds into the game by right-winger Gerry Davey, who had left his sick bed to come to the game. Davey had emigrated from Canada to England with his mother at the age of 16, but not before learning to play hockey in, incredibly, Port Arthur.

Foster, for his contribution, played the 2–1 victory brilliantly and allowed only three goals during the entire tournament. The International Ice Hockey Federation controversially reversed its original rules and announced that the second round's results would carry over to the final round. Canada was deprived of the chance to play Great Britain again, and the "second Canadian team" went on to capture the gold medal, an upset equivalent to the United States' 1980 "Miracle on Ice."

Ahearne, the architect of the English team, eventually became president of the IIHF and continued to regularly battle Canadian authorities over playing style and the use of former professionals.

WEILAND

1971

Despite his jersey not being adorned with a "C," Cooney Weiland was the captain of the 1938–39 Boston Bruins; it was his last NHL season. Weiland and the Bruins defeated the Toronto Maple Leafs in five games to capture the franchise's second Stanley Cup.

Cooney Weiland

PHARMACY'S LOSS TURNED into one of hockey's great gains.

When 19-year-old Ralph "Cooney" Weiland left his hometown of Seaforth, Ontario, to go to school in Owen Sound, Ont., his intention was to play a little junior hockey, then go on to a career as a druggist. But after leading the Owen Sound Greys to the Memorial Cup in 1924 — scoring a remarkable 33 goals in nine regular-season games and 37 goals in 15 playoff games — Weiland was in such demand as a hockey player that he never did get that pharmacy degree. He did, however, eventually commit a large part of his adult life to education, becoming a coaching legend at Harvard University.

The Boston Bruins found both Weiland and Cecil "Tiny" Thompson playing for the Minneapolis Millers of the American Hockey Association and signed them for the 1928–29 season. The two rookies played key roles for the Bruins, propelling the club to its first Stanley Cup victory that season. Weiland had a respectable 11 goals and 18 points in the 40-game schedule, but it was in the following season, when the league relaxed its restrictive forward-passing rules, that Bruins fans were treated to one of the most astonishing regular seasons in NHL history.

With Aubrey "Dit" Clapper and Norman "Dutch" Gainor joining him on the Dynamite Line, Weiland shattered Howie Morenz's single-season scoring record by a phenomenal 43 percent. His 73 points were 22 better than Morenz's previous mark and included 43 goals, just one short of the magical goal-a-game mark. Clapper chimed in

with 41 goals, and the Bruins went 38-5-1 in the regular season, at one time winning 14 games in a row (an NHL record that stood until the 1982 New York Islanders won 15 straight). But despite Weiland leading all playoff scorers, the Montreal Canadiens swept the Bruins in the Stanley Cup final to cut short Boston's bid to win back-to-back Cups — something that hadn't been accomplished since the Ottawa Senators won in 1920 and 1921.

In 1932 the Senators purchased Weiland. However, the club was in serious financial decline and had to sell him to the Detroit Red Wings less than two years later. By 1935 Weiland was back in Beantown, where he spent the final four years of his playing career.

The Bruins won their second Stanley Cup in 1938–39. It was Weiland's last season, and it was in the sweater pictured here that he helped the Bruins dust the Toronto Maple Leafs in five games. Upon retirement, Weiland went behind the bench as a coach to begin his second, much lengthier hockey career. After piloting the Bruins to their third Cup victory in 1940–41 he then spent six years coaching in the American Hockey League before taking over the hockey program at Harvard in 1950. Weiland coached at Harvard for 21 years, retiring in 1971, the same year he was inducted into the Hockey Hall of Fame.

At Weiland's funeral in 1985 one of his Harvard players delivered a eulogy praising his coach as one of the greatest influences in his life and asserting that Harvard became one of the world's leading institutions because of its teachers, one of whom was Weiland.

Twenty-five years later, that player, David Johnston, was named the governor-general of Canada.

Shane Doan wore this Kamloops Blazers jersey for the 1994–95 Western Hockey League season and the 1995 Memorial Cup, where he recorded nine points to lead the tournament in scoring and capture MVP honors. The Blazers defeated the Detroit Junior Red Wings 8–2 to capture their third Memorial Cup in four years.

Shane Doan

IT WOULD BE impossible to choose the best Canadian major junior hockey team of the 20th century, but the 1994–95 Kamloops Blazers would certainly be high on any list of candidates.

The Blazers were the wire-to-wire leaders in that remarkable season, ranked number one among Canadian Hockey League teams from their first game right through to their last, an 8–2 rout of the Ontario Hockey League's Detroit Junior Red Wings in the Memorial Cup final.

That Memorial Cup tournament was played in Kamloops, British Columbia, but the Blazers were no back-door entry as the host team. They had opened the season with four straight wins to run their Western Hockey League record to 33 consecutive regular-season victories and closed it with five straight victories, including their sixth-game clincher against the Brandon Wheat Kings in the WHL final and an unblemished 4–0 record in the Memorial Cup.

The 1994–95 season saw the Blazers win their second straight Memorial Cup (their third in four years) as well as their sixth WHL championship and 10th Western Division title in 12 years. The 1995 Memorial Cup was also the fifth by the Blazers and their ancestors, the most by any WHL franchise.

The Blazers began as the Humboldt Indians of the Saskatchewan Junior Hockey League in 1946. The club eventually moved to Estevan, Saskatchewan, and then to New Westminster, B.C., where, as the Bruins, they won their first two Memorial Cups. In 1981 the franchise was transferred to Kamloops, where they were the Oilers for three years and then took on the Blazers nickname in 1984. In their first 31 years in Kamloops, the team missed the playoffs only twice.

The 1995 Memorial Cup–winning team brimmed with future NHLers, including Tyson Nash, Brad Lukowich, Darcy Tucker (who was their regular-season and playoff scoring leader in the back-to-back Cup years), Jarome Iginla (who was the 1995 Memorial Cup's most gentlemanly player) and Shane Doan (who was the Most Valuable Player of that home-ice Memorial Cup).

It was 18-year-old Doan's third and last season in Kamloops. That June he was taken seventh overall in the NHL draft by the Winnipeg Jets. Doan ended up becoming the Jets' final first-round choice as the club moved to Phoenix after the 1995–96 season, Doan's rookie year.

In 1994–95, Doan's final season with the Blazers, he registered 37 goals, 94 points and 106 penalty minutes — a preview of the kind of rugged, steady-scoring, two-way game he would bring to the NHL. However, it took him a while to acclimate.

After managing no more than six goals in any of his first three seasons, Doan burst into prominence with the Phoenix Coyotes in 1999–2000 when he scored 26 times for the first of nine straight seasons of 20 or more goals. He also reached the 30-goal plateau twice in that stretch.

Doan, who was named the Coyotes' team captain in 2003, was the last of the Jets to still play for Phoenix, and he quickly became the indisputable face of the franchise. He was also a regular and productive member of Canada's national teams, winning silver medals at the 2005 and 2008 World Championships and gold medals in 2003 and 2007, when he was team captain.

When Canada won the 2004 World Cup just prior to the NHL lockout, Doan scored the winning goal in Canada's 4–2 victory over Finland in the gold-medal game.

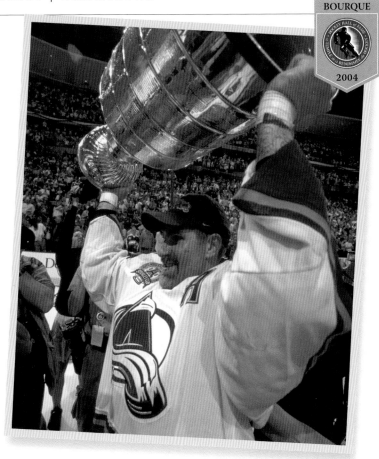

Ray Bourque wore this jersey during the second period of Game 7 in the 2001 Stanley Cup final. After 40 minutes of play, the Colorado Avalanche retired to the dressing room with a 3–1 lead they would not relinquish, finally earning Bourque a Stanley Cup after 22 seasons.

Ray Bourque

THE GESTURE SAID SO MUCH about the two men, each of them a captain to the bone.

On June 9, 2001, Joe Sakic's Colorado Avalanche beat the New Jersey Devils 3–1 in the seventh game of the Stanley Cup final. But when the Colorado captain accepted the Cup from NHL commissioner Gary Bettman, he ignored the NHL's traditional rhythm and neither hoisted the Cup, nor skated it around the arena. Instead he passed it over to his assistant captain to perform those happy rituals.

And 22 seasons, 214 playoff games and 1,612 regular-season games after he entered the NHL, Raymond Bourque finally held the Stanley Cup in his talented hands.

Sakic's unselfish move underscored the esteem which the entire hockey world held for Bourque, who was an uncommonly complete player with spectacular offensive skills and the most accurate shot in hockey, and who was also one of the best and fiercest defenders in the game.

There was joy in Colorado, and even — and perhaps especially — in Boston, where Bourque had played for 21 years and captained the Boston Bruins for 15, the longest tenure in franchise history. With Boston he scored a goal in his first NHL game in 1979, was named Rookie of the Year, went on to win five James Norris Memorial Trophies, and was personally and professionally respected league-wide. But despite joining the Bruins during their pro-sport record string of 29 straight playoff appearances, the closest he came to the Stanley Cup were losses to the Edmonton Oilers in the 1988 and 1990 finals.

Boston general manager Harry Sinden traded the talented defenseman to Colorado toward the end of the 1999–2000 season — ignoring Bourque's request to go to an Eastern Conference team — largely because he thought the Avalanche had a better chance at winning a Cup than any team in the East.

However, the Avalanche lost to the Dallas Stars in the seventh game of the conference final that year, with Bourque hitting the post on a late-game shot which could have forced overtime. But in 2000–01, with Patrick Roy in net; Bourque, Rob Blake and Adam Foote anchoring a brilliant blue line; and Sakic and Peter Forsberg leading the forwards, the Avalanche could not be stopped. They finished first overall in the league by a whopping 12 points, swept the Vancouver Canucks in the first round of the playoffs, then beat the Los Angeles Kings and St. Louis Blues to win the Western Conference.

Game 7 of the Stanley Cup final was Bourque's last in uniform and he went out on top, not only with his team, but also as an individual. Twenty-two years after he became the first rookie position player to be selected to the First All-Star Team, he was named a First All-Star again and was runner-up for the Norris Trophy. He also held the NHL career records for goals, assists and points by a defenseman.

Bourque started his career in Boston wearing No. 7, the number made famous in Beantown by none other than legend Phil Esposito. During the 1987 Boston Garden ceremony to honor Esposito, Bourque peeled off his sweater to reveal his new No. 77 so that Esposito's famous No. 7 could be retired.

Fourteen years later he found himself on the other end of an equally unselfish gesture.

RICHARD

1979

Henri Richard wore this Montreal Canadiens jersey in Game 7 of the 1970–71 Stanley Cup final versus the Chicago Black Hawks where he scored both the game-tying and Cup-clinching goals. It was Montreal's 16th Stanley Cup and Richard's 10th.

Henri Richard

IT DIDN'T TAKE LONG FOR Henri Richard to go from living in a huge shadow to casting one of his own.

When Henri Richard joined his older brother Maurice "Rocket" Richard on the Montreal Canadiens in the fall of 1955, there were widespread assumptions that the 19-year-old made the team only as a pacifier to the franchise legend. Elmer Lach, the Rocket's legendary line-mate, had even told the younger Richard that he would never be an NHL player, despite coaching him during a superlative junior career.

The "Pocket Rocket," as Henri was known, always insisted that his primary goal was to make the Canadiens in time to play with his brother. Maurice himself said he likely would have retired much earlier had he not had the chance to play his final five seasons with Henri, who was 15 years his junior.

But the younger Richard bore excellent credentials even before proving from the opening day of training camp that he belonged in the NHL at the age of 19 — an extremely early debut for a Canadiens' player of that era. Henri had won the Quebec junior scoring title with the Junior Canadiens the two previous years and, while he was short and slight, unlike his muscular brother, he was a crafty puckhandler and playmaker. Henri scored big goals, fore-checked like he was possessed and could acquit himself well in a fight. In 1960, his older brother's last hurrah, Henri led all playoff scorers with 12 points, helping the Canadiens become the first NHL franchise to win five straight Stanley Cups.

Henri was a Stanley Cup winner each of his first four years in the NHL, and before he retired he had hoisted the Cup 11 times — the most championships won by any NHL player, as well as any professional team athlete. (Bill Russell of the NBA's Boston Celtics shares this record.) He led the league in assists twice, and he scored two Stanley Cup–winning goals: one in 1966 in overtime and another when he wore this sweater, notching the deciding marker in the 1971 Stanley Cup final.

The 1970–71 season was a tumultuous one for the Canadiens, and their Cup victory behind rookie Ken Dryden's goaltending is considered one of the larger surprises in their deep reservoir of titles. It was the last year of the dynamic one-two punch of Henri and Jean Beliveau, and upon Beliveau's retirement Henri assumed the Canadiens captaincy for the final four years of his career.

After missing the playoffs in 1970 for the first time in 22 years, and the only time in Henri's career, the lightly regarded 1970–71 Canadiens beat the heavily favored Boston Bruins in the first round and won the seventh game of the Cup final over the Chicago Black Hawks 3–2, despite falling behind by two goals. Henri, benched by coach Al MacNeil earlier in the series, scored twice in the comeback, including the winner. He later said of the Cup win, his 10th, that it "was the best because we were such underdogs it wasn't funny."

Veteran Montreal broadcaster Dick Irvin Jr. may have put it best when he described the Canadiens' spring as being "just like fiction."

TRETIAK

1989

No. 20 sweater worn by goalie Vladislav Tretiak, during the 1973 World Championship in Moscow. Tretiak posted a stellar 1.80 goals-against average as the Soviets went undefeated to claim the gold on home ice. At right, Tretiak is shown during the 1972 Summit Series.

Vladislav Tretiak

TO CANADIAN HOCKEY FANS, he was the enemy they just couldn't hate.

And Vladislav Tretiak felt the same way. His one unfulfilled hockey dream was to play in the country he had twisted into knots during the 1972 Summit Series for the team that celebrated that country in its very name.

The Montreal Canadiens selected Tretiak in the seventh round of the 1983 NHL draft, and general manager Serge Savard (who had played against and been frustrated by Tretiak in the Summit Series) was confident he could get the world's greatest goalie to Montreal after the 1984 Sarajevo Olympics.

But the Union of Soviet Socialist Republics' government resisted, which, when added to Tretiak's distaste for USSR national coach Viktor Tikhonov, pushed him into retirement at the premature age of 32.

Just prior to that first series between the full-time USSR "amateurs" and NHL players in 1972, Team Canada scouts had identified the 20-year-old Tretiak as the exploitable weakness of a team no one really knew. Not realizing he had been celebrating his impending wedding the previous evening, the scouts were misled by an eight-goal landslide the only time they saw him play. But after letting in two early goals in the first game, Tretiak spent the rest of the series demonstrating why he would eventually be voted the International Ice Hockey Federation's all-time goalie.

The Canadiens regularly outshot the Soviets, but they trailed the series throughout six games largely because of Tretiak. Even with

their country's hockey reputation being eroded, Canadians across the country came to appreciate that it was the confidence the Russian players had in Tretiak that allowed the USSR to be so selective in the few shots they took.

Tretiak cemented his iconic status in what many Canadians still consider the greatest game ever played: New Year's Eve 1975, the Montreal Canadiens versus the CSKA Red Army. The touring Soviets were outshot that night 38–13 and still escaped with a 3–3 tie because of Tretiak's wizardry.

Although the USSR had some of the best players in the world, Tretiak became the international face of Russian hockey during the eight-game Summit Series of 1972, and remained there for 14 years when he was the Soviet league's top goalie. He assumed his mantle again in 2006 when he became head of the Ice Hockey Federation of Russia.

Tretiak saved his best for international competition, where his goals-against average was a miniscule 1.78, which was nearly his average in the 1973 World Championship. On the same Palace of Sports ice where Paul Henderson had finally solved Tretiak only six months earlier, Tretiak allowed only 18 goals in 10 games as the USSR outscored their opposition 100–18 to claim the world title.

Tretiak is the only Russian player to compete in four Olympics, in which he won three gold medals and one silver. That silver came in 1980 when the USSR lost the "Miracle on Ice" after Tretiak was pulled for allowing an American goal in the final seconds of the first period.

Tikhonov later said it was the worst coaching decision he'd ever made. Tretiak, and the rest of the hockey world, had to agree.

New York Islanders jersey worn ▶
by Clark Gillies throughout the
1979–80 NHL season, including
the playoffs, where the Islanders
defeated the Philadelphia Flyers
in six games to capture their first
of four consecutive Stanley Cups.

Clark Gillies

"I'M NOT SURE POWER FORWARD was a term we were using back then," says legendary New York Islanders defenseman Denis Potvin. "But that's exactly what he was. He was 6-foot-3, 215 pounds and he got 38 goals. Amazing."

Clark Gillies, the left-winger Potvin had succeeded as captain, was a master at creating space for himself and for Bryan Trottier and Mike Bossy, his two artistic accomplices on the legendary Long Island Lighting Company Line — named for its propensity to keep the goal light lit — which fronted the four-year Islanders Stanley Cup reign.

In February 1977, three years into his professional career, the 22-year-old Gillies became Islanders captain, replacing Ed Westfall, the franchise's original team captain. Despite scoring 35 times in each of the next two seasons and recording his highest point total (91) in 1978–79, Gillies wasn't fully at home with the "C." After the Islanders were upset by the Toronto Maple Leafs in the 1978 quarterfinal and by the New York Rangers in the 1979 semifinal, Gillies passed the captainship to Potvin just prior to the 1979–80 season.

Captain or not, Gillies complemented the extraordinary skill set of the Long Island Lighting Company by working the corners as well as any winger in the league, setting bulky, immovable screens in front of the net, using his hard shot from the low slot and fighting just enough to keep the opposition wary.

"You really had to push him," says Rick Dudley, who went on to manage several NHL teams after a 10-year playing career. "I remember my first game after I got back to Buffalo from the World Hockey Association in 1978 and wanted to make an impression. I kind of ran Gillies a few times, but he didn't seem interested in fighting me. I did

notice, though, how big he was. Then in the playoffs, I saw he and Terry O'Reilly going at it and I was *really* glad he didn't want to fight me that day. He was a powerful guy."

In 1980, on the way to the first of their four straight Stanley Cups, the Islanders got past O'Reilly's Boston Bruins in the quarterfinal, with Gillies doing much of the physical work up front as the Islanders finally came of age after several years of playoff disappointments. That series win was followed by a six-game series victory over the Buffalo Sabres in the semifinal, highlighted by a Bob Nystrom double-overtime goal in Game 3.

In the Stanley Cup final against the first-place Philadelphia Flyers, who had established an NHL regular-season record of 35 straight games without a loss, Nystrom scored again in overtime of Game 6 to give the Islanders their first Cup. Gillies, for his part, played in all of the Islanders' 21 playoff games, collecting six goals (two of which were game winners) and 10 assists to go along with his career-high 63 playoff penalty minutes.

While a late-season deal to obtain center Robert "Butch" Goring from the Los Angeles Kings was justifiably credited with helping the Islanders finally get over the top of their playoff struggles, general manager Bill Torrey had assembled the core of the club through the amateur draft: Nystrom in 1972; Potvin in 1973; Gillies and Trottier in 1974; and Bossy in 1977. The exception was goaltender Billy Smith, who was taken in the 1972 expansion draft after having played only five games for Los Angeles the previous year. Smith and Nystrom were the only Islanders from the 1972 inaugural season still in uniform for the franchise's first Stanley Cup.

Jim Paek assisted on Ron Francis' Cup-winning goal while wearing this jersey in Game 4 of the 1991–92 Stanley Cup final. The jersey features a patch to honor the late Penguins coach Robert "Badger Bob" Johnson, under whom the club won their first-ever Stanley Cup the previous season.

Jim Paek

R OBERT "BADGER BOB" JOHNSON said international hockey would be good for Jim Paek's game, and two Stanley Cups prove he was right.

In the fall of 1990, after three years of toiling with the International Hockey League's Muskegon Lumberjacks, Paek finally made the Pittsburgh Penguins and became the first Korean-born player in the NHL. But the Penguins were a team loading up for the Stanley Cup, and Paek was sitting in the press box too often.

"So Badger Bob sent me to the Canadian National Team," Paek recalls. "He had all those ties to the American national program, and I think that had a great influence on him sending me there.

"It was tremendous. You got experience playing against some of the world's best players, and you'd practice 20 or 30 days in a row before going over to Europe, so you were developing your skills," Paek continues. "And you couldn't ask for better coaches than Dave King, Perry Pearn and Wayne Fleming."

Paek never expected Johnson's late-winter call. "We were in some little town in British Columbia, and Bob said: 'We're calling you up for the playoffs.' I was going to be the ninth defenseman, and Bob's advice was 'Enjoy yourself and you never know what could happen.'"

What could happen, did happen: Three starting Pens defensemen were injured, and Paek — promoted from insurance policy to sixth defenseman — played well in his eight games, scored his first NHL goal and became the first Korean player to win the Stanley Cup.

Johnson died in November 1991 from brain cancer, and with Scotty

Bowman behind the bench as his replacement the Pens repeated as Cup champions in 1992. Paek was often scratched during the season, but he was a regular in the playoffs and even assisted on the Cup-winning goal.

"They were both very special teams, and it started with Badger Bob," says Paek. "He was a special man — very positive — and it filtered down through the entire group. What character guys we had on that team, and future Hall of Famers, too: Mario Lemieux, Jaromír Jágr, Paul Coffey, Bryan Trottier, Larry Murphy, Ron Francis. Tom Barrasso was also incredible in goal."

Paek was born in Seoul, South Korea, but immigrated with his family to Toronto when he was only a year old and eventually fell in love with the Canadian game.

"But you never forget where you come from," he says. "You still look back and see yourself as Korean, and that what you've accomplished makes other Koreans proud. We had a little Stanley Cup parade in [Toronto's] Korean Town when we won."

While Paek was playing for the Oshawa Generals in the mid-1980s, he and his brother started a hockey team for Korean-Canadians that traveled to Seoul and Chicago for games and cultural experiences. He has also conducted coaching clinics in his birth land.

"The first time I went back to Korea, in 1982, they didn't have any hockey except at university and high school," says Paek. "No club teams, nothing at elementary school. Now they have it all.

"I don't know if I can take any credit for it," he continues, "but at the time the Penguins won, hockey really started to grow in Korea. And now they've got the 2018 Winter Games."

JAMES
2010

Pink, blue and white jerseys worn ▶
by the first-ever true Canadian
Women's National Team during
the inaugural International Ice
Hockey Federation Women's
World Championships. Team
Canada, led by captain Sue
Scherer (left) and top-scorer
Angela James (right), routed the
competition by a combined score
of 61–8 to capture the gold.

Trailblazers

IT WASN'T QUITE THE RIGHT COLOR scheme for hockey pioneers who were smashing the international gender barrier.

The first official Women's World Hockey Championship, held in Ottawa, Ontario, in 1990, was marked not only by its groundbreaking status, but also partly by the much-maligned pink uniforms worn by Team Canada.

"It was kind of a 'powder puff' type of thing," Angela James recalls with an air of forgiveness. "But at the time we were just so happy to play in a world championship that we would have worn anything. You could finally play for your country. It was just an ecstatic time for all of us."

It was particularly euphoric for veterans of the women's game — such as James and Sue Scherer, whose jerseys are depicted here — who had elevated the play of women's club and postsecondary school teams to unprecedented heights, but who could advance no further than the national championship.

Often referred to as "the Wayne Gretzky of women's hockey," James played both defense and center. She possessed speed, finesse and a wicked slap shot, all of which helped her become the Ontario college Most Valuable Player three years in a row while playing for Seneca College. James went on to score 33 goals and 51 points in 50 games for Canada's national team, winning gold in the first four world championships. Much of her career she was connected to the North York Aeros, a legendary Toronto team that helped substantially raise the bar for women's club-team hockey. With the Aeros, James won national titles in 1991 and 1993, and the team was a charter member of the National

Women's Hockey League, the first women's professional league. Her Aeros sweater is also housed at the Hockey Hall of Fame.

Scherer was a two-time Ontario university All-Star for the University of Guelph Gryphons and a superb all-around athlete who represented Canada at world championships in two different sports: softball and hockey. She was a catcher for the Canadian women's softball team, which finished fifth at the 1982 Worlds and fourth in 1986. She also backstopped the club to gold medals at the 1981 and 1983 Pan American Games. Scherer also won gold for Canada at the first two Women's World Hockey Championships.

At the inaugural Worlds, Scherer was Canada's captain, while James was the offensive juggernaut, scoring 11 times in the tournament — a Canadian single-tournament record that still stands. Canada, wearing its whites, beat the United States 5–2 in the 1990 final for its first of eight-straight gold medals; the U.S. finished runner-up each time.

In 2008, James, her national teammate Geraldine Heaney, and Cammi Granato of the U.S. were the first women named to the International Ice Hockey Federation Hall of Fame. And two years later, James and Granato became the first women enshrined in the Hockey Hall of Fame — signposts of the evolution of women's hockey.

"In the past, 95 percent of the players in any arena would be boys," says James. "Now it wouldn't be a surprise to see two of the four ice pads with girls or women on them. Everything that is available to boys is now available to girls, and the dynamics of parenthood have changed. It's not just 'Take your boy to the arena' anymore."

Czech Republic alternate captain ▶
Jaromír Jágr, shown at the 2010
World Championship, wore this
jersey at the 1998 Winter Olympics
in Nagano, Japan – the first Games
with NHL participation. Jágr led his
team in scoring with five points,
and the Czechs won their first-ever
Olympic gold in hockey.

Jaromír Jágr

DESPITE HIS FAMILY HISTORY, and despite the number he wore on his back, Jaromír Jágr insists that it wouldn't have mattered who the opposition was.

"Not at all," he says. "I just wanted to win. Who we played didn't make any extra difference."

But for so many of his Czech Republic countrymen, the 1–0 victory they scored over Russia in the gold-medal final of the 1998 Winter Olympics was, and still is, a historical signpost.

With the fall of the Iron Curtain, Slovakia and the Czech Republic eventually went their separate political ways after decades of forced amalgamation as Czechoslovakia. The hockey win at Big Hat Arena in Nagano, Japan, was the first Winter Olympic gold medal for the reborn nation.

More deeply, every time the Czechs defeated Russian or Soviet Union teams the victory dripped with defiant symbolism. Prior to the Soviet Bloc's dissolution in the early 1990s, Czechoslovakia had been under the direct influence of the Union of Soviet Socialist Republics. The Soviet Union had dispatched tanks to quell the 1968 Prague Spring rebellion, the darkest moment in the country's history. Although he wasn't born until four years later, Jágr had always worn the No. 68 to commemorate both the uprising and the death of his grandfather the same year. His grandfather had been jailed by the Soviets for opposing the takeover of his farm, and died in prison.

Coming into the first Olympic tournament to have the full participation of the NHL, Jágr and the Czechs were massive underdogs behind Canada, the United States and Russia.

"Nobody ever gave us any chance before the tournament, but we knew we had the best goaltender in the world," says Jágr, who has more NHL goals, assists and points than any other European-trained player. "And our goal was just to play good defense. I think the coaches and management did a really good job picking the team. They picked half from Europe and half from the NHL, and that makes a huge difference when you play on the big ice."

With perennial All-Star goalie Dominik Hasek at the peak of his game, the Czech Republic beat the U.S. team 4–1 in the quarterfinal, then shocked Canada in the semifinal with a 2–1 victory that needed a five-per-side shootout to decide. Robert Reichel scored the winner while Hasek blanked all five Canadian shooters. Many Canadian hockey fans were left to ask "What if?" as coach Marc Crawford controversially did not include Wayne Gretzky among the five shooters.

That propelled the Czechs into the gold-medal game against Russia, 30 years after the tanks rolled into Prague. Russia had beaten the Czech Republic 2–1 in the preliminary round, but in the gold-medal final, Jágr (who scored only one goal in the tournament but eschewed individual stats for a team system) and his teammates applied a defensive tourniquet. Russia could not solve Hasek, and 12 minutes from the end of regulation time Petr Svoboda's slapper from the blue line gave the Czechs the lead, and consequently their first-ever Olympic hockey title.

More than 150,000 emotional admirers were waiting at the Prague airport when the team returned to their still-new republic as national heroes.

Seve Bobrov, seen at right in the top row holding a trophy in a team picture, wore this blue sweater when he and his country shocked the world by winning the 1954 World Championship – the first time the USSR had ever entered the tournament. Bobrov was named the tournament's top forward.

Seve Bobrov

IT WAS A MUTUAL ADMIRATION society, open only to "Rockets."

Vsevolod "Seve" Bobrov, who didn't even see a game of hockey until he was 23, felt honored to be nicknamed "The Russian Rocket" in homage to the Montreal Canadiens' Maurice "Rocket" Richard, four decades before Pavel Bure earned the same title. And Richard had always said that Bobrov was one of the top 10 players in the history of hockey.

However, while Bobrov's goal-scoring statistics were overwhelming, it would be just as fair to compare him to Lionel Conacher and his supreme athleticism as to the Rocket and his explosive sniping. Bobrov not only captained the Union of Soviet Socialist Republics hockey teams to their first World and Olympic championships, he was also the country's leading soccer goal-scorer for several years and scored a hat trick during the 1952 Summer Olympics. He also represented the USSR in bandy, the stick-and-ball skating game.

Bobrov was the captain of the Soviet team that entered the World Championship for the first time in 1954 in Stockholm. It was less than a decade after the USSR had started to take the game seriously, and Canada had already won 15 world titles. But when the Soviets played the Canadian representative, the East York Lyndhursts, in the final game of the Worlds, they jumped out to a 4–0 first period lead and didn't let up.

The Lyndhursts were a Senior B team that had made it to Stockholm because the Allan Cup–winning Kitchener-Waterloo Dutchmen (and other Senior A teams) didn't want to underwrite the growing financial demands of representing Canada abroad (which was customarily done by the Allan Cup champion). Still, the Lyndhursts had outscored the

opposition 52–10 in the first six games of the tournament and needed only a tie with the USSR to come home with gold.

The Soviets didn't look like much of a threat, striding onto the ice wearing bicycle helmets and sweaters that were too long for them while carrying homemade sticks. But they had trained brutally hard under fierce coach Anatoli Tarasov and had fully analyzed the Canadian playing style. On soft afternoon ice in front of 16,000 fans in an outdoor soccer stadium, the Russians completely outclassed the Lyndhursts from the opening minute.

"Their slowest player was faster than our fastest player," Lyndhurst player Eric Unger said famously.

As the game wore on the Russians continued to apply pressure and they won the gold handily with a shocking 7–2 victory.

Twenty-eight years later in a motivational speech before the first game of the famous 1972 Summit Series, Bobrov, who was then coaching the USSR, showed his nervous team a photograph from 1954.

"It shows me, the captain, sitting at a desk like a schoolboy while a Canadian lectures me on hockey," Bobrov said. "Then we beat them 7–2. Do not be afraid."

Bobrov was the cornerstone of early USSR hockey, playing on seven Soviet championship winning teams and scoring 254 career goals in just 130 league games for three Moscow teams. He, Yevgeny Babich and Viktor Suvalov formed the first great line in Soviet hockey history, and anyone who scores 250 career goals in Russia is now inducted into the Bobrov Club.

So, with the NHL initiating the Maurice "Rocket" Richard Trophy in 1999, both Rockets from the 1950s have modern goal-scoring honors named after them.

Bobbi-Jo Slusar wore this ▶
University of Wisconsin Badgers
jersey for the program's first
national championship at
the 2005–06 Women's Frozen
Four tournament.

Bobbi-Jo Slusar

BOB HICKMAN HAS SEEN it all evolve. Quickly.

Hickman, the director of women's hockey operations for the University of Wisconsin Badgers, was a Wisconsin student and a volunteer team manager with the Badgers when they were walloped 8–1 by the University of Minnesota Duluth Bulldogs in their first-ever league game in 1999.

The women's division of the Western Collegiate Hockey Association — and most of its teams — was in its first year when UMD visited the Kohl Center in Madison, Wisconsin, that fall to play the Badgers and open the schedule in front of 3,891 people.

"We got a little reality check," recalls Hickman, who has enjoyed the reality a lot more since then.

By the 2005–06 season, when First Team All-American and former University of Notre Dame Hounds star Bobbi-Jo Slusar wore this sweater, the Badgers were a national force. They won their first of back-to-back WCHA and National Collegiate Athletic Association titles, and became the first team not only to record a shutout in the women's Frozen Four tournament, but to blank both their semifinal and final opponents.

Behind stellar defense led by the mobile puck-moving Slusar, Badgers goalie and Wisconsin native Jessica Vetter shut out the St. Lawrence University Saints 1–0 in the NCAA semifinal, as well as the two-time defending champion University of Minnesota Golden Gophers 3–0 in the final, which was held right in Minneapolis.

Slusar led the NCAA in scoring by a defenseman in 2005–06, registering 12 goals and 28 assists for 40 points over 39 games. For her efforts she was named the WCHA's Defensive Player of the Year and earned a nomination to the WCHA All-Tournament Team.

The 2005–06 Wisconsin hockey season was the most complete that any American college program has ever enjoyed. The women won Wisconsin's first women's NCAA title of any kind in 21 years, the men's Badgers won their first NCAA hockey championship in 16 years, and Wisconsin became the first school ever to win both men's and women's hockey titles in the same season.

Adding an exclamation point to an already remarkable season, both the men's and women's champions boasted a member of the Burish family, from hometown Madison. Nikki Burish and future NHLer Adam Burish were the first siblings to play for national champions in the same year.

The Badgers have since gone on to win three more national titles, with Slusar — who eventually played internationally for Team Canada — acting as captain of the 2006–07 Wisconsin squad that finally exacted full revenge on the Bulldogs with a 4–1 decision in the Frozen Four final, retaining their NCAA supremacy.

The program had come a long way since 1998, when the women's Badgers consisted of exactly one player: red-shirted goalie Jackie MacMillan, who practiced with the men's teams and welcomed recruits to campus as the team prepared for the inaugural WCHA season the following year. The league was already planned, but the women's hockey gold medal at the 1998 Olympics "threw gasoline on the fire," Hickman says.

In the Badgers' fourth year, the "Johnson magic" arrived when Mark Johnson — a star of the 1980 "Miracle on Ice" and son of famous men's coach Robert "Badger Bob" Johnson — took over as women's head coach.

"No one else in the women's game has the incredible experience of playing in the NHL, world championships and Olympics," says Hickman.

◄ Speedy right-winger Mike
Gartner wore this jersey while
participating in the 1975 Wrigley
National Tournament in Oshawa,
Ontario. Gartner's Barrie Co-ops
defeated the reigning champion
Verdun Maple Leafs 7–4 to earn
the national title.

Mike Gartner

BY THE TIME Mike Gartner and Viacheslav Fetisov were inducted into the Hockey Hall of Fame, international hockey exchanges between Russia and Canada had become commonplace, and the pair had played against each other dozens of times in the NHL and on the world stage. But 26 years earlier, when the two superstars first shared the same ice — unbeknownst to each other at the time — games between Canadian and Soviet teams were still novel.

"We didn't realize until the day we were inducted into the Hall that we'd played against each other in 1975," says Gartner, who was an underage player with the Barrie Co-ops when they earned the right to tour the former Soviet Union.

From 1974 to 1978 the Wrigley National Midget Hockey Tournament brought together the top midget-aged teams from across Canada with the winner earning a trip to the Union of Soviet Socialist Republics for games against midget and junior teams. The Verdun Maple Leafs won the inaugural event and their 6–5 loss to the Red Army reportedly attracted 100 million viewers on one of the only two TV stations in the USSR.

The next year, Barrie was the upset winner with two future NHLers in the lineup: goalie Doug Keans and the fleet-footed Gartner.

"You didn't get national championships in minor hockey very often back then," Gartner recalls. "Barrie had a population of only 25,000, and we were in a lower category than all the other [teams], so we had to make a special application to get in. I was a minor midget and called up for the last few games."

The early 1970s saw the best of the NHL narrowly defeat the Soviet National Team in the 1972 Summit Series, and the 1974 Soviets easily handled the World Hockey Association All-Stars in a similar eight-game format.

"And the Wrigley was basically the next thing after that," says Gartner of the Co-ops' tour against HC Spartak Moscow, HC Dynamo Moscow and two Red Army teams, one of them Fetisov's.

"When we played in the Soviet Union it was the dead of winter and everybody seemed to be dressed in dark clothing. And the people were not all that friendly," says Gartner.

Wrigley's sponsorship eventually gave way to other corporate partners of the national midget tournament, and today it remains one of Canada's most important hockey events, with many future NHLers taking part at key points in their minor careers. But few graduates of the tournament can boast of success like Gartner's.

Always blessed with blazing speed, Gartner went on to record seventeen 30-goal seasons — more than any other player — and he became the fifth NHLer to surpass 700 goals. He scored the first goal in the Phoenix Coyotes' history and the last goal at Chicago Stadium. He also accomplished the rare feat of recording his 500th goal, 500th assist and 1,000th point in the same season; and when he collected his 1,000th point, against the New Jersey Devils in January 1992, Fetisov was playing for the Devils.

Gartner's career highlight was the 1987 Canada Cup, one of eight times he has represented Canada internationally, but he says he has never forgotten his very first time, as a 15-year-old.

KURRI
2001

Edmonton Oilers right-winger Jari ▶
Kurri wore this sweater during
the 1984–85 season as the Oilers
captured their second consecutive
Stanley Cup. Kurri set numerous
records this season, including the
most regular-season goals by
a right-winger (71) and the most
goals by any player in a single
playoff season (19).

Jari Kurri

JARI KURRI SET THE GOAL-SCORING standard for right-wingers, even though much of his best work happened on the left side of the ice.

"The enduring image of Jari Kurri is coming in on his off-wing, his stick poised, waiting for the perfect pass he knew was going to come, then burying it," recalls celebrated Canadian sports writer Cam Cole, who was with the *Edmonton Journal* for 23 years and covered Kurri through his spectacular decade with the Edmonton Oilers.

The perfect pass was coming, of course, from Wayne "The Great One" Gretzky. Every set-up man needs a finisher, and in Kurri (the original "Finnish Flash"), Gretzky had the perfect complement. Of Kurri's 601 career goals, The Great One assisted a stunning 364.

But Kurri was far from a one-trick pony. Many insiders consider him the most complete player of the Oilers' Stanley Cup dynasty in the 1980s. His shooting, passing (196 assists on Gretzky goals alone) and skating skills were obvious, but he was also one of the best defensive forwards of his era.

Kurri, a 20-year-old from Helsinki's famous Jokerit club, arrived in Edmonton in the fall of 1980, the Oilers' second season in the NHL. Originally reluctant to come to North America, he planned to stay only two years before returning to Finland, but he ended up playing 17 seasons and retiring as the highest-scoring European-born-and-trained player in NHL history, with 1,398 points.

He scored 32 goals in his first year and 161 throughout his first four,

before he enjoyed a season for the ages in 1984–85. On the way to a career-high 135 points, Kurri netted 50 goals in the first 50 games he played (although the Oilers had played 53 games, thus negating him from the official 50-50 club where membership dictates that 50 goals must be scored in the first 50 scheduled games). He went on to score 71 in all that year, a record for right-wingers at the time. Five years later Brett Hull broke the mark with 72 goals, and in 1990–91 Hull shattered the new mark with 86.

Kurri made the NHL First All-Star Team and also won the Lady Byng Memorial Trophy in 1984–85, but it was in the postseason that he went on a scoring rampage for the ages.

Kurri scored 19 goals to tie Reggie Leach's all-time single-season playoff record and scored 12 times against the Chicago Black Hawks in the Campbell Conference final, the most ever for a single playoff series. Nine of those goals came on three hat tricks, a record for one series, and his four hat tricks overall that spring established a new mark for most games with three or more goals.

After Gretzky was traded to the Los Angeles Kings in 1988, Kurri still recorded 1.27 points per game and helped the Oilers to a fifth Stanley Cup in 1989–90. He would later join Gretzky in Los Angeles and again with the New York Rangers.

In 1997–98, his final NHL season, Kurri also participated in the 1998 Olympics. While Finland didn't win, they did score an upset bronze medal. And it was Kurri who tallied first for Finland in their 3–2 victory against Gretzky's Team Canada for the bronze.

Harold "Boat" Hurley, shown ▶
at left with the Ontario Hockey
Association Senior Guelph
Regals in the mid-1960s, wore
this Galt Hornets sweater en
route to the 1971 Allan Cup
championship, capturing his
third Canadian national senior
title. He retired at the end of
the season.

Harold Hurley

THERE WAS A TIME in men's senior hockey when the amateur game was more important than the professional brand and when goaltenders like Canada's Harold "Boat" Hurley were better known around the world than even Terry Sawchuk or Johnny Bower.

By May of 1971 that time was drawing quickly to an end: the NHL was expanding rapidly; new professional leagues like the World Hockey Association were about to blossom; and Canada's top senior team would soon no longer represent the country at the world championship.

But in Galt, Ontario, senior hockey was still king and the Galt Hornets were head of the royal household. For the second time in two years, the Hornets played host to and swept the Calgary Stampeders to win the Allan Cup, emblematic of Canadian senior hockey supremacy.

The Allan Cup was first awarded in 1909 after the Stanley Cup became a pros-only challenge cup the previous autumn. The Galt Terriers were a senior power in the 1930s, and the popular nickname was resurrected for a new senior team in 1960.

Hurley was the goalie on that reborn Galt Terriers team, and he was fresh from a silver medal at the 1960 Winter Olympics in Squaw Valley, California, where his Kitchener-Waterloo Dutchmen had represented Canada. The Terriers won the 1961 Allan Cup, earning a berth in the 1962 World Championship in Denver and Colorado Springs, and Hurley won another silver. He was the only goalie in the tournament to wear a mask.

The Terriers folded briefly in 1962, but were reincarnated almost immediately as the Galt Hornets. In the five seasons from 1967–68 to 1971–72 the team reached the finals of the Ontario Hockey Association Senior League every year. They won the league title in both 1969 and 1971, and survived four ensuing playoff rounds to win the Allan Cup both times.

Hurley was with the Oakville Oaks in 1969, but was recruited for Galt's drive to the national championship that year. He was one of four team members still active with the club who had also won the Allan Cup with the 1961 Terriers. Both he and Joe Hogan played in both championships, while Bill "Wiggie" Wylie, who was a player in 1961, was the coach in 1969. Doc "Toots" Last was the trainer both years.

In 1971 Hurley was credited with his third Allan Cup win for Galt, though he rarely suited up for the team that year and retired at the end of the season.

Hurley personified the senior game, often referred to as "working man's hockey." A junior star in Stratford and a giant in the Ontario senior ranks, he was good enough that the Detroit Red Wings and Toronto Maple Leafs both sought to sign him for their development systems. But Hurley decided to stick it out in the senior ranks. There were only six big-league goaltending jobs available at that time, and the Leafs had Bower while the Red Wings had Sawchuk. So, like many talented players of his era, Hurley chose a career that he considered much more stable than professional hockey — accountancy — and was content to be a senior hockey legend.

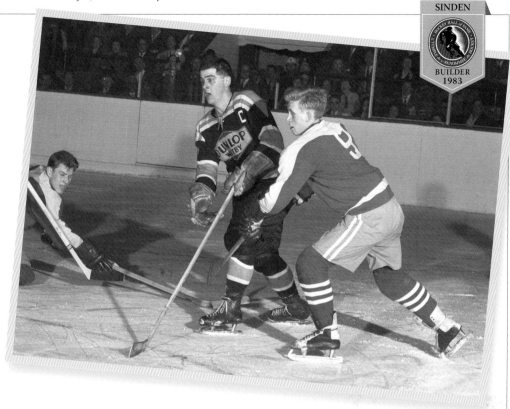

SINDEN

BUILDER
1983

Harry Sinden wore this Whitby Dunlops jersey while representing Canada at the 1958 World Championships. Milt Dunnell of the *Toronto Star*, wrote of the Dunlops and their tournament victory: "They were carrying the worries of the world on their shoulders and they played as if the world had a bulldozer on top of it."

Harry Sinden

LONG BEFORE HIS MOST renowned international hockey achievement — coaching Team Canada to the 1972 Summit Series victory — Harry Sinden was going nose to nose with the Soviet Union in major tournaments. Sinden was a smooth-passing amateur defenseman when his Whitby Dunlops boarded an ocean liner for Oslo, Norway, in February of 1958. The Dunlops, who had won the Allan Cup the previous year, were heading to the World Championship and spent six seasick days on the boat because their head coach, Wren Blair, was terrified of flying.

The Dunlops were less naive than previous Canadian contingents after the Soviets had won both the 1954 World Championship and the 1956 Olympics. Canada had then boycotted the '57 Worlds because of the Union of Soviet Socialist Republics' invasion of Hungary. The Dunlops were so serious about reestablishing Canadian supremacy that no wives or relatives were permitted to accompany the team on a trip that lasted nearly two months.

The "Dunnies" were a magnetic bunch who captured the country's imagination. Born as a Senior B team in nearby Bowmanville, Ontario, in 1953, and staffed mostly by former Oshawa Generals, like Sinden, the team was so good that by 1955 they were a Senior A team in Whitby, Ont., with sponsorship from the Dunlop Rubber Company. In 1957 they won their first Allan Cup.

Behind Sinden (the team captain), former Toronto Maple Leafs star Sid Smith (the playing coach) and local hero Bobby Attersley (who worked in the tire factory), the Dunlops breezed through a 14-game exhibition series in Europe prior to the start of the World Championship. They continued on at the same pace for the first six games of the Worlds before meeting the USSR in the final game on the outdoor ice at Jordal Amfi Stadium, where the Edmonton Mercurys had won the 1952 Olympic title.

The Dunnies received thousands of good luck telegrams from an anxious homeland — and Foster Hewitt was in Oslo to broadcast the game to Canada on radio — but things didn't start well as the USSR led 1–0 until the final minute of the second period. Then Attersley, who went on to become mayor of Whitby, delivered 21 of the most determined minutes in Canadian international hockey history. He tied the game late in the second period, then scored twice within five seconds with about four minutes remaining to give Canada the gold medal.

The Dunlops won the Allan Cup again in 1959, but turned down the chance to represent Canada at the 1960 Olympics. The Kitchener-Waterloo Dutchmen, who represented Canada at the Olympics instead of the Dunnies, picked up Sinden; they then went on to win the silver medal.

Sinden then spent six years as a player-coach in the Boston Bruins minor system before being promoted to Bruins' head coach in 1966. At 33, he was the youngest coach in the league, coaching the youngest team. With Bobby Orr and Phil Esposito dominating in 1969–70, Sinden coached the Bruins to their first Stanley Cup in 39 years. He left the club for a year, then returned as general manager for the Bruins' 1972 Cup triumph. That fall, Sinden's crew of Canadian All-Star talent beat the USSR again, if just barely.

Cassie Campbell (at left, celebrating in 2003) wore this blue Calgary Oval X-Treme jersey for the 2002–03 National Women's Hockey League season and playoffs. Danielle Goyette (at right, representing Canada internationally) wore this white Oval X-Treme jersey for the 2006–07 Western Women's Hockey League season and the 2007 Women's National Championship. From 2002–03 to 2007–08, the X-Treme won six straight championships.

X-Tremely Good

WHEN CASSIE CAMPBELL was growing up in Brampton, Ontario, she and a friend attended a hockey school run by NHLer Eddie Shack. They were the only two females on the ice.

Flash forward a couple of decades and Campbell is running her own hockey school, "and there are 300 girls registered," she says. "You feel pretty proud about that."

Especially proud, since she and "all my teammates played a little part in it," she says.

The growth of North American female hockey in the late 20th and early 21st centuries was spectacular, and stars such as Campbell and Danielle Goyette, her national and Calgary Oval X-Treme teammate, provided much-needed role models for a new, much wider, generation of players.

And the Oval X-Treme "was our version of an NHL team," says Campbell. "We played full time, we were on the ice for two hours a day, and we played maybe 60 games a year, counting national team games."

Because the Canadian Olympic team had gathered in Calgary prior to winning its first Olympic gold medal at Salt Lake City, Utah, in 2002, and many players stayed in Calgary afterward, the X-Treme was able to put together an enormously talented roster for the inaugural season of the National Women's Hockey League in 2002–03, which is when Campbell wore this blue sweater.

"That was our best team," says Campbell, who captained the X-Treme as well as the 2002 and 2006 Olympic champions. "We had so much fun and so many good players, like Danielle and Hayley [Wickenheiser]."

The X-treme won the NWHL championship in both years of its short existence, then won four straight Western Women's Hockey League championships before losing in the final in 2009, their club's final year of existence. In its last five seasons the Calgary powerhouse boasted a staggering 95-3-2-1 record.

While Campbell retired before the 2006–07 season, Goyette played another year before leaving the ice to concentrate on coaching the University of Calgary Dinos women's team. Goyette also left the national team as its all-time leading goal-scorer, with highlights that include being the top tournament goal-scorer at the very first Olympics that included women's hockey in Nagano, Japan, in 1998, as well as tying for the goal-scoring lead at the 2002 Salt Lake Olympics — the site of Canada's first women's hockey Olympic gold.

Goyette was Canada's flag bearer for the opening ceremony at the 2006 Olympics in Torino, Italy, and Campbell, for the second straight Games, captained the team to a gold medal.

"Her style as a leader was more outgoing than people before her and she brought a lot of visibility to the game," says Hayley Wickenheiser of Campbell. "She's been a great role model for female hockey players."

"I don't think women's hockey had a face," Campbell reluctantly concedes, "and that came with the territory of being captain at the time when women's hockey was getting so much attention because of the Olympics. But there were so many other women before me that were groundbreakers."

She thought female hockey was on the right track with the national league, but the short life span of the Oval X-Treme indicated how much work there is still to do.

"Women's hockey is big, but it's still not there yet," Campbell says. "We always have to fight for our leagues and our teams."

The inaugural New England Whalers season established green as the basic color for the uniform and the stylized "W" as a franchise staple. Terry Caffery can be seen at right modeling the original road uniform. The harpoon in this sweater was later replaced because of cultural sensitivity to the cruelty of the whaling industry.

Terry Caffery

STABILITY WAS A WORD seldom heard during the tumultuous seven-year life of the World Hockey Association. But there was a relative steadiness to the New England Whalers.

From the very beginning the Whalers were a regional team, clearly stressing local appeal and cornerstone players — which is what allowed the franchise to survive and prevail, despite playing in three different cities and four different arenas over the seven years the WHA existed. The club played their first two years in Boston, at both the Boston Bruins–owned Boston Garden and in the old Boston Arena. They played their third season in Springfield, Massachusetts, and moved to Hartford, Connecticut, for good in 1974, which is where the club remained when it joined the NHL in 1979. (The New England Whalers became the Hartford Whalers when they joined the NHL at the insistence of the Boston Bruins.)

Originally denied entry to the new league during the first wave of the WHA recruitment, a Boston-based partnership finally landed a WHA franchise three weeks later on November 1, 1971. One of the owners was Howard Baldwin, who at 28 was one of the youngest executives in professional sport at the time — he'd later be named president of the WHA.

The Whalers made immediate inroads in the New England market by making hard-nosed Ted Green from the Bruins their first captain; appointing Boston University legend Jack Kelley as head coach; bringing in more American-trained players than other teams; and making their first signing Larry Pleau of Lynn, Massachusetts, who had won a Stanley Cup with the Montreal Canadiens. Plus, their Whalers nick-name honored a primary local industry while constantly reminding fans, with its first three letters, of the new league.

While many WHA teams opted for headline-grabbing contracts, the Whalers went for a little more permanence, building from the crease out with former Pittsburgh Penguin Al Smith in net and a trio of young Toronto Maple Leafs products — Jim Dorey, Rick Ley and Brad Selwood — on the blue line.

But it was the offense that powered the Whalers to win the Avco Cup in the WHA's inaugural championship of 1973, a five-game victory over the Winnipeg Jets, who were the other consistently stable franchise in the league's brief life.

Despite the focus on defense and American players, it was a pair of forwards from Ontario who powered the Whalers to the leading goal total in the WHA's first season. Playing on a line with former Leafs player Brit Selby, fellow Toronto Marlboros grad and hustling center Terry Caffery became the first Whaler to reach 100 points. Right-winger Tom Webster cracked the century mark a few days later and established the then-franchise record of 103 points. Webster was also the dominant scorer in the playoffs, with 26 points in just 15 games.

Caffery was named the WHA's first Rookie of the Year, but a knee injury he played with during the playoffs forced him to miss the league's entire second season and to retire within two years. That curtailed a promising career that had included a Memorial Cup and a year with the Canadian National Team.

The debut season helped establish the continuity the Whalers sought from the beginning: Pleau played and coached with the franchise until 1989; and Ley, Webster, Selwood, Pleau and Tom Earl all played over 350 games with the Whalers.

Joseph Sullivan

THEY WERE SO GOOD TOGETHER, they couldn't let graduation break them up.

In February 1928, on an all-purpose outdoor rink in the spectacular alpine setting of St. Moritz, Switzerland, a group of former University of Toronto students known as the Toronto Varsity Grads completed the final leg of their unprecedented domination of world amateur hockey by steamrolling their way to Canada's third straight Olympic gold medal.

The Varsity Grads had been formed in 1926 from a core of players who had won the very first Memorial Cup championship in 1919 while playing for the preparatory University of Toronto Schools. The same core then helped the University of Toronto Varsity Blues win the 1921 Canadian university championship.

In their first year of post-graduation senior competition, the Varsity Grads won the 1927 Allan Cup, edging the Fort William Thundering Herd 2–1 in the deciding game. The victory earned the Grads the right to represent Canada at the second official Winter Olympics.

Joseph "Stonewall" Sullivan, who was studying medicine, was the number one goalie for all of those triumphs. Just before the Games he was at the center of a power play that resulted in coach Conn Smythe refusing to accompany the team to St. Moritz. Smythe, who coached the undergraduate U of T Varsity Blues team and had just bought the NHL's Toronto St. Patricks, had promised two of his university players roster spots on the Varsity Grads Olympic squad. However, Sullivan and scoring star Hugh Plaxton won a political battle to have their brothers, Frank Sullivan and Bert and Roger Plaxton, included on the team instead.

When the Grads did arrive in St. Moritz 10 days before the Olympics, their skill and speed in practice so impressed event organizers that the Canadians were given a bye directly to the medal round, while the other 10 entrants played a preliminary round to produce the other three medal contenders.

In the medal round, Canada beat silver medalist Sweden 11–0, won 14–0 over Great Britain the following day and — in their third game in as many days — clinched the gold, Canada's only medal of the Games, with a 13–0 rout over Switzerland. (The bronze medal the Swiss won was the first of only two medals the nation has ever won in Olympic hockey.)

Sullivan played the first and last game, while backup Norbert "Stuffy" Mueller guarded the goal against Great Britian. Plaxton and David Trottier led all tournament scorers with 12 goals each in just three matches.

Following a post-Olympics tour — during which the team was called the greatest hockey team ever seen in Europe — the Grads disbanded. In the two years the team played together they lost only three games.

Sullivan, who became an ear, nose and throat specialist, went on to a brilliant medical career and remained connected to U of T. In 1957 he was appointed to the Canadian Senate by Prime Minister John Diefenbaker, and one of his old teammates, Hugh Plaxton, also ended up on "the hill" as a member of Parliament, after playing 15 games for the NHL's Montreal Maroons.

Trottier, staying with hockey, starred for 10 years for the Montreal Maroons, adding the 1935 Stanley Cup to his university, Allan Cup and Olympic championships.

HOCKEY HODGEPODGE

This compilation features some of the best-of-the-rest from the vaults of the Hockey Hall of Fame.

Battle Worn & Time Tested

A COLLECTION OF WOOL SWEATERS FROM HOCKEY'S PAST — SOME FROM LONG-FORGOTTEN TEAMS AND OTHERS FROM TEAMS WHOSE LEGACIES LIVE ON STRONG

PREVIOUS PAGE: St. Louis Eagles sweater worn by Frank Finnigan in the franchise's lone NHL season in Missouri (1934–35) after many prodigious years as the Ottawa Senators.

TOP LEFT: Moose Jaw Canucks sweater (Saskatchewan Junior Hockey League, 1946–47) worn by Harvey Stein.

TOP RIGHT: Selkirk Fishermen sweater (Manitoba, circa 1930s), player unknown.

BOTTOM LEFT: Calgary Canadians sweater (Alberta Junior Hockey League, 1929–30) worn by Les Moss while winning the Sandercock Cup.

BOTTOM RIGHT: Edmonton Flyers sweater (Western Canada Senior Hockey League, circa 1947–48) worn by Stephen "Bingo" Murluk during the club's Allan Cup championship.

Minor-Professional Threads

THE MINOR-PROS ARE HOCKEY'S CROSSROADS, WHERE FUTURE AND FORMER NHLERS CROSS PATHS WITH CAREER-MINOR LEAGUERS, ALL PLAYING THE GAME THEY LOVE

PREVIOUS PAGE: Phoenix Roadrunners jersey worn by Bruce Boudreau in 1989–90 for the inaugural season of the International Hockey League. Boudreau recorded his 500th professional point in this jersey.

TOP LEFT: Cleveland Lumberjacks jersey (IHL, 1999–2000) worn by Jock Callander when he recorded his 1,383rd IHL point to become the league's all-time leading scorer, including playoffs.

TOP RIGHT: Fort Wayne Komets jersey (IHL, 1968–69) worn by Len Thornson in his last professional season. Thornson finished as the IHL's all-time points leader with 1,337 points, including playoffs.

BOTTOM LEFT: Des Moines Oak Leafs jersey (IHL, circa 1964), player unknown.

BOTTOM RIGHT: Kansas City Greyhounds jersey (American Hockey Association, 1937–38) worn by Eddie Bush.

Making Waves

THE TRAILBLAZERS AND HEROES OF WOMEN'S HOCKEY

TOP LEFT: Jersey worn by Finnish star Sari Krooks at the 1997 Women's World Championship in Canada where her team took home bronze.

TOP RIGHT: Jersey worn by Geraldine Heaney in 2003–04, her final National Women's Hockey League season. Heaney retired as a national champion when she scored the overtime winning goal for the Abby Hoffman Cup.

BOTTOM LEFT: McGill University Martlets jersey worn by goaltender Kim St. Pierre when her team won the 2000 Women's Canadian Interuniversity Athletic Union championship where she took home the Most Valuable Player honors.

BOTTOM RIGHT: Minnesota Whitecaps jersey worn by Julie Chu for the 2009–10 Western Woman's Hockey League season. The Whitecaps captured the Clarkson Cup and Chu was named tournament MVP.

FACING PAGE: Preston Rivulettes sweater worn by Hilda Ranscombe during the 1930s. The Rivulettes, led by Ranscombe, were Canadian champions for the entire decade, losing only two of 350 games.

Oh Canada

SOME OF THE MANY JERSEYS WORN TO REPRESENT CANADA INTERNATIONALLY

PREVIOUS PAGE: The white Team Canada jersey worn by Rod Seiling in the 1972 Summit Series is surrounded by the red '72 jerseys worn by Canadian savior Paul Henderson and tournament extras Bobby Orr and Michel "Bunny" Larocque.

TOP LEFT: Advertisement-adorned jersey worn by goalie David LeNeveu while representing Canada at the Spengler Cup in 2009. Starting in 1984, Canada became the only national team to compete at this club-team tournament.

TOP RIGHT: Jersey worn by Mike Moller while representing Canada at the 1982 World Junior Championship, where the team captured the nation's first-ever World Junior gold medal and Moller walked away as the tournament's MVP.

BOTTOM LEFT: A departure from the traditional red and white, this jersey was worn by Pierre Larouche while representing Canada at the 1977 World Championship.

BOTTOM RIGHT: Jersey worn by sledge hockey superstar Billy Bridges while leading Canada to a gold medal at the 2006 Paralympic Games.

Acknowledgments

I would like to thank the staff of the Hockey Hall of Fame — especially Phil Pritchard, Craig Campbell, Miragh Bitove, Steve Poirier, Izak Westgate, Darren Boyko and Kelly Masse — for providing me with contacts and allowing me access to the Resource Centre to conduct research, I really felt at home. Thanks to the players who took the time to discuss their old sweaters, the book would not be the same without you. I'd also like to thank Hal Roth and Jamie Hodgson, the book looks great! Special thanks to Steve Cameron at Firefly Books for his steady hand.

As always, my eternal gratitude to Jess, Toby, Nora, Karen, Josh, Michelle and my pal and lifelong teammate Thumb, who wore all the same old sweaters as me.

—Steve Milton, author.

Working on *Hockey Hall of Fame Book of Jerseys* was a great thrill, and it would not have been possible without the contributions of the following people, whom I would like to recognize and thank:

Steve Milton, for your words! You tell fantastic stories. It is a joy to get lost in my work, which is what happens when I read your stuff.

Hal Roth, for your dedication to making great images. Your patience and keen eye were essential in making the jerseys come to life on the page. Thanks for your positive attitude and easygoing nature, you were a joy to work with.

Phil Pritchard, Craig Campbell, Miragh Bitove, Steve Poirier, Izak Westgate, Kirt Berry, Anna Presta and Bill Wellman at the Hockey Hall of Fame Resource Centre, as well as Peter Jagla, Craig Baines, Tome Geneski, Tyler Wolosewich, Scott Veber and Pearl Rajwanth at the Hockey Hall of Fame. Thank you for your patience, knowledge and support and for providing me ready access to the collection.

Jamie Hodgson, for your great design. From beginning to end, you've managed to capture exactly what I envisioned for this book.

Special thanks to: Edward Kowal, Beth Zabloski and Ron Hutton; as well as to Lionel Koffler, Michael Worek, Jacqueline Hope-Raynor, Hartley Millson, Jolie Dobson, Nicole North and the rest of my great colleagues at Firefly Books.

Lastly, thanks to the rest of the staff of the Hockey Hall of Fame: Bill Hay, Jeff Denomme, Ron Ellis, Darren Boyko, Kelly Masse, Jackie Schwartz, Wendy Cramer, Joshua Dawson, Joanna White, Craig Beckim, Steve Ozimec, Patrick Minogue, Dwayne Schrader, Mike Briggs, Sarah Lee, Anthony Fusco, Sandra Walters, Chris Chu, Arlyn Fortin, Sylvia Lau, Sarah Talbot and the maintenance crew (especially those who stayed overnight on photo shoots).

—Steve Cameron, editor.

Photo Credits

Index